Intelligent Business

Workbook

Intermediate
Business English

| Louise Pile |

Pearson Education Limited
Edinburgh Gate
Harlow
Essex CM20 2JE
England
and Associated Companies throughout the world.

www.longman.com

First published 2005

ISBN 0 582 846919 (with audio CD)

Set in Economist Roman 10.5 /12.5

Printed in Spain by Graficas Estella

Acknowledgements

The publishers are grateful to The Economist for permission to
adapt copyright material on page 6 (©2003), page 11 (©2003), 13
(©2004), page 17 (©2003), page 19 (©2003), page 24 (©2003), page 29
(©2004), page 32 (©2003), page 33 (©2003), page 35 (©2003), page 41
(©2003), page 43 (©2003), page 45 (©2003), page 51 (©2003), page 56
(©2002), page 58 (©2003), and 61 (©2003). All material copyright of
The Economist Newspaper Limited. All rights reserved.

We are also grateful to the following for permission to reproduce
copyright material: Keith Uren Publishing for an extract from Isle
of Man Portfolio Magazine Issue 40, 2003
www.portfolio@manx.net; Coventry Evening Telegraph for an
extract from the article 'Managers Dream of a Perfect Place to
Work' 3rd June 2003; and NI Syndication for an extract from the
article 'Firms Do Better When Workers Take Control' published in
Sunday Times 14th September 2003 © The Times 2003.

Photograph acknowledgements

Alamy/D.Gray p37; Corbis/M.Yamashita, J.F. Raga p50, B.Varie p52;
Getty Images/Stone p14, K.Reid p34, C.Furlong p57, Hulton Archive
p61; Kellog School/T. Duncan p5; Lugano Hotels/ K. Hayden p13;
Panos Pictures/M. Henley contents page (t), p21; Press
Association/EPA/A. Gombert p20, EPA p49; Reuters p43, T. Melville
p30; Rex Features/ P. Cooper contents page(b), p51, Sipa p58; Zefa/L.
Williams p38, K. Davies p42, Pinto p47, D. Lim p54, MTPA Stock
pp59, 63.

Every effort has been made to trace the copyright holders and we
apologise in advance for any unintentional omissions. We would
be pleased to insert the appropriate acknowledgement in any
subsequent edition of this publication.

Front cover images supplied by Corbis (left and right) and Apple
Computer, Inc. (centre).

Picture Research by Sally Cole.

Illustrated by John Bradley

Designed by Cathy May

Contents

Development
What is the OECD?

The Organisation for Economic Cooperation and Development (OECD) brings together the governments of the more economically developed countries to exchange ideas and discuss economic policy. How much do you know about its objectives and services? **Page 21.**

Lobbies
Striking the right balance

Recent European Commission plans to regulate the chemicals industry are seen as a minor victory by lobbyists but European producers complain they will be at a competitive disadvantage and warn of the dangers of excessive legislation. With the greens saying the plans don't go far enough, the battle looks set to continue in the European Parliament and Council of Ministers. **Page 51.**

Unit 1 Companies

Vocabulary: Companies
Language: Present simple and present continuous
Career skills: Talking about your job
Writing: Email changing arrangements

Vocabulary

1 Use the clues to find the words in the puzzle.

1 relating to companies
2 client
3 joining together of two companies
4 someone who starts their own business
5 involving too much administration /paperwork
6 linked chain of companies or individuals
7 arranged according to rank or status
8 owner of shares in a company
9 company that provides resources for another company

1								C	O	R	P	O	R	A	T	E		
2								O										
3								M										
4								P										
5								A										
6								N										
7								I										
8								E										
9								S										

2 Complete the sentences with *by, for, of, on, to* or *with*.

1 Shares in corporations are usually sold ___*on*___ the Stock Exchange.
2 One advantage _____ working for TBF is the career structure.
3 Who is responsible _____ staff development in this department?
4 The key _____ survival for most companies is flexibility.
5 Companies need to be able to adapt _____ a changing environment.
6 A team of ten people reports _____ the IT Manager.
7 Many companies used to provide workers _____ lifelong employment.
8 The Head of Procurement is in charge _____ purchasing.
9 Traditional companies are being replaced _____ networks of companies working together.
10 Which division deals _____ issues related to patents?

1 Listen to the first part of a radio programme about the Kellogg School of Management. The speaker refers to three types of company and student. Make notes on them below.

	type of company	type of student
1	Large international corporation	All senior staff paid to attend
2		
3		

2 Which areas of work do students at Kellogg come from?

3 What other areas of work within a company can you think of?

1 Now listen to the second part of the programme. Make notes below on how Kellogg has responded to challenges facing the business school.

challenges facing Kellogg	changes to courses at Kellogg	other changes at Kellogg
Tough business school market (number of job placements and starting salaries for MBA graduates). No automatic top job offers.		

2 Match the pairs from the radio programme.

1 business   a resources
2 social   b school
3 human   c salary
4 starting   d company
5 start-up   e responsibility
6 customer   f services

1 Complete the article below with the following sentences.

a To put a good idea effectively and profitably into practice generally requires managerial experience and authority.

b He does not mean that firms should set up their own 'universities' – although plenty, from Motorola to McDonald's, have done that.

c Universities everywhere are largely state-financed.

d They are all hugely successful: there are far more of them, and far more students, than ever before.

e Certainly, there are aspects of the university that firms might envy.

f For example it gathers, under a single powerful brand, individuals contracted to supply it with their intelligence.

The Economist

Business education

What might the company of the future look like?

Companies and universities: a little learning

Lawrence Summers, president of Harvard University, suggests in the latest Harvard Business Review that the American research university, eg Harvard, might be a model for the company of the future. 1 ___b___ Instead, they should adopt the research university's fluid and decentralised approach to creativity and hierarchy. "If you look at the organisations in the economy where the greatest value is being added," argues Mr Summers, "they are increasingly the organisations that share the values and character of universities."

2 _____ They are, to start with, extraordinarily durable institutions. Mr Summers' own Harvard, founded in 1636, is very young compared with the University of Bologna, founded in 1088, or Paris and Oxford born less than a century later.

3 _____ In the rich world alone, 39m people are now taking a university course of one sort or another. And they teach more subjects than ever before. Anyone tempted to mock McDonald's Hamburger University should look at the classes in food technology and catering that plenty of modern universities now provide.

The successful university has other characteristics that firms increasingly aspire to. 4 _____ Moreover, the deals struck by the most successful academics when they transfer from one university (often European) to another (usually American) are becoming more lucrative, with all sorts of perks regarded as normal.

But there is one big difference that Mr Summers does not mention. 5 _____ Harvard's students may pay for their teaching, but the university's research, which Mr Summers urges firms to copy, is subsidised with public money.

Public support gives most universities a financial stability that companies do not enjoy. Sure, companies succeed on the back of big ideas, but on the whole it is their application that makes money. 6 _____ That is why clever 25-year-old graduates rarely run durably successful companies, even if they are from Harvard.

Language check	**1** Match each question about jobs with an appropriate answer below. Then decide how you would answer each question.

1 What's your job?   `b`

2 What does that involve? ☐

3 How long have you been in your present job? ☐

4 Do you enjoy your work? ☐

5 Is there anything you don't like about your job? ☐

6 How do you spend your time when you're not working? ☐

a I've worked here for about four years now.

b I'm a supervisor in a logistics company called Express Move.

c I enjoy team sports like rugby, but I don't play as regularly as I'd like.

d Well, the role involves bureaucracy – and I'm not very keen on that!

e Very much. My job entails a lot of different tasks – from co-ordinating drivers to liaising with suppliers – so I don't get bored.

f I'm responsible for 13 warehouse staff and report to the site manager.

2 Complete the emails with the correct form (present simple or continuous) of the verbs in brackets.

From: samwakely@nhn.com

To: narinderbarr@nhn.com

subject: Can we arrange to meet?

Dear Narinder

I (¹write) _____'m writing_ to ask if we can meet to talk about plans for the new IT system. Everything (²be) _____ fine here in general. But we (³currently/ have) _____ problems with saving data. The developers (⁴know) _____ about the problems but can't find a solution – so we (⁵think) _____ the launch date will need to be postponed. I was going to suggest that we meet on Friday 3 June as I (⁶usually/see) _____ Steve Barker at your office one Friday a month. But I (⁷understand) _____ that you (⁸not/work) _____ Fridays. So how about Monday 23 May? By the way, what's it like coming back to work after maternity leave? (⁹imagine) _____ it must be difficult when the baby is so young. She (¹⁰look) _____ lovely in her photo. Anyway, let me know if Monday 23rd would suit you.

Regards

Sam

Writing	You are Narinda. You cannot meet Sam on the day he suggests. Write an email (40–50 words) to Sam:

– explaining you cannot meet when proposed and giving reasons

– telling Sam when you will be free

– suggesting another time and date

– offering to arrange a meeting room.

Then compare your answer with the suggested answer on page 90.

Unit 2 Leadership

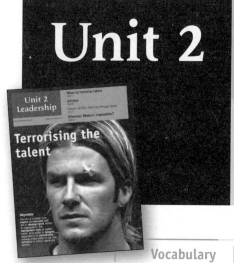

Vocabulary:	**Leadership**
Grammar:	**Articles**
Career skills:	**Getting things done**
Writing:	**Email making a request**

Vocabulary

1 Use the clues to find the words in the puzzle.

1 special ability
2 time limit
3 give someone work to do
4 have control over
5 appreciated
6 motivate

1			T	A	L	E	N	T			
2				E							
3				A							
4				D							
5				E							
6				R							

2 Complete the sentences with *on, in, by, into, to, with* or *of*.

1 Janice is very good at dealing ___*with*___ problems in the workplace.
2 The manager needs to take control _____ the situation immediately.
3 If management aren't careful, staff will go _____ strike.
4 A friend of mine recently asked me to go _____ business with him.
5 Today's management session will focus _____ marketing strategies.
6 Managers need to make company information more accessible _____ staff.
7 I don't think a good leader is someone who rules _____ terror.
8 A good leader should be open _____ new ideas.
9 What do you think is needed to succeed _____ business?
10 I'd say your way of managing staff is similar _____ mine.

3 Match the verbs and nouns.

1 take   a a balance
2 attend   b a risk
3 strike   c an example
4 set   d a problem
5 resolve   e an event
6 found   f a company

4 Now use the verb and noun pairs to complete the sentences.

1 Managers find it hard sometimes to strike a ___balance___ between being too informal and too formal with their employees.

2 How many company events do you have to _____ every month?

3 My supervisor always works late – I think he wants to _____ an example.

4 How did you manage to _____ the problem?

5 Good leaders are rarely afraid to _____ risks.

6 My colleague has decided to _____ his own company.

5 Which is the odd one out in each set?

1 **a** manager	**b** chief executive	**c** subordinate	**d** leader
2 **a** precedent	**b** success	**c** limit	**d** target
3 **a** achieve	**b** reach	**c** meet	**d** lose
4 **a** reduce	**b** improve	**c** develop	**d** increase
5 **a** deadline	**b** cost	**c** expectation	**d** dismissal
6 **a** positive	**b** trusted	**c** poor	**d** valued
7 **a** fire	**b** motivate	**c** reward	**d** inspire
8 **a** risk	**b** consensus	**c** position	**d** chance

6 Complete the tips for effective leadership below with the following verbs.

develop   lose   take   set   give   make   resolve   dominate   avoid   create

Tips for effective leadership

1 ___Resolve___ any problems quickly.
2 _____ care to involve staff.
3 Always _____ clear instructions.
4 _____ unrealistic targets.
5 Do _____ sure your staff feel valued.
6 _____ talent among your staff.
7 _____ your temper.
8 _____ causing stress among workers.
9 _____ a positive working environment.
10 Lead meetings but _____ them.

Look at the use of articles (*a*, *the* or no article at all) in the sentences. Only three sentences are correct. Identify the correct sentences and find and correct the mistakes.

1 I have *a* job in a leading design company.
2 Gabi Hart is director.
3 A manager is not the same as leader.
4 Employees don't want to be led; they want to be managed.
5 Does the fear really motivate people to do better in their work?
6 Most managers learn from the experience.
7 Bob is one of youngest managers here but he's also one of the best.
8 Culture can affect attitudes to management.
9 Newspaper article I read on the train this morning was very positive about management today.
10 I don't know of many really strong leaders in the world at the moment.

1 Six people talk about the qualities of successful leaders. Listen and match each speaker with one of the qualities.

a Ability to develop talent   ☐
b Self-confidence   ☐
c Ability to take unpleasant decisions   1
d Clarity of thought   ☐
e Ability to judge people   ☐
f Effective communication skills   ☐

2 Now use adjectives from the audioscript on pages 80–81 to complete the sentences.

1 It's important for a manager to give c *lear*_____ instructions to staff.
2 Business isn't simple: managers have to be prepared to deal with c_____ situations.
3 There are no standard solutions; managers need to find the most e_____ solution for each particular situation.
4 All leaders are asked to deal with c_____ demands – so they need to be able to prioritise.
5 A good manager develops his /her team and isn't j_____ of other people's success.
6 Flexibility is c_____; without this quality, no manager can survive.

1 Read the article about choosing a leader. It contains twelve proof-reading mistakes. Find and correct them.

The Economist

Business

Leaders

Tough at the top

Choosing a leader

used

So, are companies worse than they ~~use~~ to be at chosing good leaders? Certainly, given the importence of the top job, companies sometimes appear to select their leaders in unsatisfactory ways. They rarely advertise for a boss or select anyone from another country (apart from in Britain, were 32 of the cheif executives of the FTSE 100 firms are not British).

Moreover, they rarely appoint anyone who has been the CEO of another large public company. Of course, sucessfully picking a leader has always been tricky because the job requires at last two quite different skills. Like the fox, a CEO must know lot of little things and must manage the key day-to-day aspects of the business. But like the hedgehog, he must also know one big thing: every three or for years, he will have to take a substantial strategic decisin, wich may fatally damage the busness if he gets it wrong. Plenty of giants, such as Cable & Wireless and AT&T, have had leaders who passed the fox test but failed the hedgehog one.

MANAGER

2 Franz has written an email to a colleague. Rewrite Franz's email using a softer approach to ensure that he gets things done. Then compare your answer with the suggested answer on page 90.

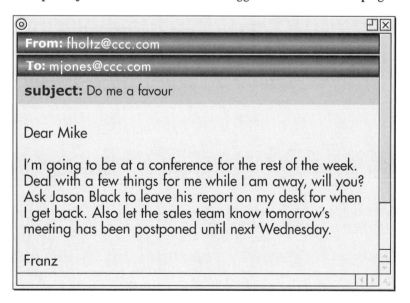

From: fholtz@ccc.com

To: mjones@ccc.com

subject: Do me a favour

Dear Mike

I'm going to be at a conference for the rest of the week. Deal with a few things for me while I am away, will you? Ask Jason Black to leave his report on my desk for when I get back. Also let the sales team know tomorrow's meeting has been postponed until next Wednesday.

Franz

Unit 3 Strategy

Vocabulary: **Strategy**
Language: **Future forms**
Career skills: **Short presentations**
Writing: **Email agreeing to give a presentation**

Reading **1** What do you already know about Giorgio Armani? Make notes under the following headings. Then read the article on the opposite page and add further information to the notes.

current sectors of activity	proposed new sector	advantages of this strategy	risks of this strategy
haute couture *everyday clothes*			

2 Look at the article again. Seven other designers are mentioned. Who are they? Make notes on their activities.

	designer	activities
1	*Donatella Versace*	*Designed a hotel in Australia*
2		
3		
4		
5		
6		
7		

3 Match the pairs from the article.

1	fashion	a	venture
2	head	b	designer
3	brand	c	cycle
4	joint	d	goods
5	property	e	campaign
6	economic	f	developer
7	luxury	g	office
8	advertising	h	dilution

The Economist

Business

Breaking into new markets

Should luxury goods firms go into the hotel business?

GIORGIO ARMANI is already one of the most diversified brands in fashion. As well as haute couture and everyday clothes, Mr Armani and his firm create scent, cosmetics, spectacles, watches and accessories. Customers can purchase Armani furniture, flowers, chocolate, sweets, jam and even marmalade. There are Armani cafés and restaurants in Paris, New York, London and other cities. An Armani night club recently opened in Milan. Now Giorgio is branching out still further. On February 22nd his firm announced a $1 billion hotel venture with Dubai's Emaar Properties, the Middle East's largest property developers. Mr Armani will be in charge of the design for ten new hotels and four luxury resorts, to be built in the next six to eight years.

Armani's is the boldest move so far by a luxury goods company into the hotel business. But it is by no means the first. In September 2000, a hotel designed by Donatella Versace opened on Australia's Gold Coast. In February 2001, Bulgari, an Italian jeweller, confirmed a joint venture with Ritz-Carlton to build six or seven hotels and one or two resorts. Salvatore Ferragamo, an Italian shoemaker, has designed four hotels in Florence.

But in the first half of last year, both the fashion and travel industries were doing badly as travel and luxury follow the same economic cycle. So does it make sense for designers of luxury goods to go into the travel business? Armani and Bulgari would say yes. Mr Armani considers hotels a logical extension of his aim of promoting his brand in all walks of life. (So can Armani toilet paper be far behind?) Rita Clifton, Chairman of the consultancy Interbrand, says that this strategy can work. A strong product, strong images and a strong experience, such as staying at a fashion designer's hotel, can combine to make a super-strong brand, claims Ms Clifton. To fit the firm's luxurious image, Bulgari says that its hotels must be as upmarket as it is possible to be. Because small is considered more exclusive, Armani and Bulgari plan to launch mostly smallish five-star hotels. Armani's Dubai hotel, due to open in 2007, will be an exception, however, with 250 rooms. Bulgari's Milan hotel will have no more than 60 rooms.

Losing control of their brand is the biggest risk for luxury firms expanding abroad or venturing into a new line of business. Over the years, Pierre Cardin, Yves St Laurent and Christian Dior have each lost their good names by giving out licences all over the world to firms that did not deliver the appropriate quality. Calvin Klein's current problems are related to the company's loss of control of the distribution of its products in many countries.

But designers' hotels can generate positive publicity. Even if Bulgari's hotels turn out not to make any money, the venture could be seen as an expensive yet effective advertising campaign.

Mr Armani's hotel plans are more ambitious and the danger of brand dilution much greater. Armani says that the management company for its hotel venture will have its head office in Milan rather than Dubai and that Mr Armani will be fully in charge of design. So far Mr Armani has managed to control his brand tightly despite being involved in many different businesses. Hotels, however, are a bigger challenge than flowers and marmalade.

Writing You have been asked to give a presentation at a local business forum on 3 July about strategic planning. Write an email (40–50 words) to Mr Jacobs, head of the forum:

- agreeing to give the presentation
- giving the title of your presentation
- saying what equipment you need.

Then compare your answer with the suggested answer on page 00.

Listening 1 ⊙ T5 **1** Put the words in the correct order to make presentations phrases. Then listen to an extract from the presentation about strategic planning and tick the phrases that you hear.

1 to like I'd finally you remind that
   Finally, I'd like to remind you that
   _____

2 start talk I before my just to I'd thank like
   _____

3 my brings this me to next point
   _____

4 found have hope I you my useful comments
   _____

5 any have if you questions be I'll to happy them answer the at end
   _____

6 this can slide on next you see
   _____

2 Now look at the audioscript on page 81. Find words with similar meanings.

1 goals *objectives*
2 possible _____
3 expansion _____
4 dangers _____
5 evaluation _____

6 allows _____
7 possibilities _____
8 vital _____
9 successful _____
10 rivals _____

1 Underline the correct future forms in italics.

1 The department *'s going to allocate* /*allocates* more resources to the project than intended in future.

2 We *hold* / *'re holding* a strategy meeting next Wednesday.

3 I *'ll be* / *'m going to be* happy to answer any questions later.

4 The company *will meet* /*is meeting* all its objectives by spring.

5 Sorry, I can't talk now. I *'ll call* /*call* you back later.

6 The next plane *will leave* /*leaves* at 11.03.

7 I *begin* / *'m going to begin* my talk by looking at successful strategies.

8 What *will you do* /*are you doing* tomorrow evening?

9 Looking at the high level of demand, we *aren't going to have* /*aren't having* enough resources.

10 Let me move on now and I *come* / *'ll come* back to that point later.

2 Read the email about arranging a meeting. Complete the email with the correct future form of the verbs in brackets.

From: ckeough@datadrive.com

To: mjones@bhj.com

subject: Change of plan

Dear Martin

Thanks for your feedback on the business plans. I (^{1} pass) ___*'ll pass*___ your ideas to the head of department. I (^{2} see) _____ him tomorrow morning as we (^{3} have) _____ a last minute meeting to discuss the plans further. The meeting (^{4} start) _____ at 11.00 and probably (^{5} not /finish) _____ until 1.30 at the earliest. This means that I'm afraid I (^{6} not /be able to) _____ meet you for lunch as we originally planned. Can we meet another day instead? What (^{7} you /do) _____ on Thursday? I (^{8} give) _____ a presentation to a client in the morning but I (^{9} be) _____ back by lunchtime. I think the train (^{10} get) _____ in at 12.50. Let me know if Thursday is OK.

Anyway, I (^{11} phone) _____ you this afternoon.

Regards

Christine

---

1 Match each of the following nouns with one set of verbs.

resources   a strategy   customers   an opportunity   an objective

1 develop   *a strategy*
  design   _____

2 identify   _____
  take

3 set   _____
  achieve

4 allocate   _____
  provide

5 attract   _____
  draw in

Unit 4 Pay

Vocabulary: **Executive pay**
Language: **Present perfect and past simple**
Career skills: **Evaluating performance**
Writing: **Job advertisement**

Reading | **1** Read the magazine extracts about the pay of top executives. Underline the words and phrases related to their remuneration.

The spotlight rarely falls on the <u>basic salaries</u> of top executives because these do not tend to rise at such a dramatic rate. In 2002, the median <u>base salary</u> of the CEOs of the S&P 500 companies was $925,000. The median total compensation for that year, on the other hand, was $3.65m.

Charles Conaway, the chief executive of Kmart, a US discount retailer, left the company in March 2002 after just 21 months in the job and two months after the company had filed for Chapter-11 bankruptcy. A company loan of $5m, granted as part of Mr Conaway's pay package, was 'forgiven' upon his departure.

The bosses of American Airlines were revealed to have placed $41m in a pension fund for themselves that was fully protected should the company go into Chapter-11 bankruptcy. This self-appointed perk remained hidden until after negotiations with the airline's unions aimed at securing wage concessions of up to $2 billion had ended a few months later.

Trevor Fetter, Mr Barbakow's successor at Tenet Healthcare, was granted two shares in the company for every one that he purchased, up to a limit of 200,000. Many such awards of shares are in the form of 'restricted stock', which the executive is not allowed to sell for a specific period.

2 Now find the following numbers in the extracts above. What does each number refer to?

1   $925,000   *the median (average) base salary of the CEOs*
2   $3.65m
3   200,000
4   $41m
5   21 months
6   $5m

1 Match the words with the definitions.

1	golden hello	a	right to buy / sell specific shares
2	bonus	b	large sum paid to a new employee
3	pension	c	highly paid executive
4	stock option	d	money given when a contract is officially ended
5	fat cat	e	extra money paid, usually as a reward
6	remuneration	f	payment made to retired people
7	severance pay	g	pay in the form of salary and extra benefits

2 Complete the article with the correct options a–d.

The Economist

Business

Fat cats feeding

Executive pay

So-called 'golden parachutes', i.e. large pay-offs even when top executives ^{1}___*fail*___, have become a main focus this year in the debate over executive pay. The Corporate Library, an organisation set up to protect the rights of shareholders in America, believes that the average departing CEO in that country receives a severance ^{2}_____ worth $16.5m.

In May this year, shareholders at the annual general meeting of GlaxoSmithKline (GSK) protested against the amount promised to its boss, Jean-Pierre Garnier, if he were forced to leave the company prematurely. Since one of the more likely reasons for such a departure would be poor ^{3}_____, the $35.7m farewell gift was seen to be excessive.

Under new rules allowing shareholders to ^{4}_____ each year on British firms' plans related to executive ^{5}_____ GSK's owners gave it the thumbs down, which sent a shock through ^{6}_____ Britain. Yet it did not actually change Mr Garnier's package. The decision is only advisory.

Sir Christopher Hogg, the chairman of GSK, points out that the company was already undertaking a review of its ^{7}_____ policy. That review is still going on and Sir Christopher says whatever the result, "we will be seeking shareholders' ^{8}_____ at the AGM in 2004." He has written to the Association of British Insurers to say that "the board has registered shareholders' particular sensitivity to payments on termination."

British union leaders want shareholders' votes on executive pay to be made binding. And they want shareholders to register more concern about this ^{9}_____. Despite all the ^{10}_____ made over Mr Garnier, GSK remains the only company in Britain this year whose financial report failed to meet with its shareholders' approval.

---

	a		b		c		d	
1	a	lose	b	fail	c	trip	d	miss
2	a	account	b	package	c	option	d	dividend
3	a	acting	b	operation	c	performance	d	behaviour
4	a	vote	b	choose	c	elect	d	propose
5	a	income	b	turnover	c	proceeds	d	compensation
6	a	financial	b	executive	c	corporate	d	official
7	a	remuneration	b	reward	c	refund	d	repayment
8	a	admiration	b	endorsement	c	sponsorship	d	justification
9	a	theme	b	factor	c	argument	d	issue
10	a	protest	b	quarrel	c	doubt	d	fuss

1 **How would you decide what remuneration to offer a new CEO? Listen to part of a business school seminar about CEOs' pay and complete the sentences.**

1   Decisions about the salary level of a new CEO are often made by ...

   a selection committee and recruitment consultant.

2   The new CEO's salary is decided in the following way: ...

3   The risk of this kind of approach is that ...

4   A recent report revealed that ...

5   The remuneration packages of CEOs might become more acceptable if ...

2 **Check that you understand the following words about executive selection. Then listen again. Which three words or phrases are not in the tapescript?**

trend	industry	average	pay package
remuneration	salary	consultant	peer
procedure	turnover	tenure	vacancy
choice	appointment	golden parachute	contract
scandal	position	benchmarking	compensation
employee	shareholder	committee	share option
golden hello	selection	comparison	

Writing   Look at the notes in response to Harry's request and write the advert. Then compare your answer with the suggested answer on page 92.

> Please could you write a very brief job advert for the Area Sales Manager position to send to Jane at TER Recruitment (the online recruitment agency that we use). Mention the following:
>
> • base salary —— *better than average!*
>
> • bonus ————————— *depending on how well you do*
>
> • pension —— *good*
>
> • anything else you think is important.
>
> Thanks
>
> Harry
>
> *working conditions?*
> *location?*
> *how to apply?*

1 Complete the sentences using multi-part verbs with *in*, *up*, *down* and *off*. Which of the multi-part verbs take an object?

1 I'm still shocked. The realisation hasn't sunk ____*in*____ yet.

2 The CEO has stepped _____ from his position due to the company's recent poor performance.

3 We've been working for weeks to set _____ a deal with a former competitor.

4 Unfortunately, the negotiations broke _____ after just a few hours.

5 Shall we call _____ the meeting as it no longer has any purpose?

6 One of my colleagues hasn't turned _____ for work in ages.

2 Put the words in the correct order to make sentences evaluating the performance of a project.

1 deadline /the /too /was /tight   *The deadline was too tight.*

2 has /not /as /it /been /expected /easy /as

3 month /final /up /we /catch /managed /the /in /to

4 into /have /they /run /a /problem

5 deadline /sure /not /the /I /am /I /will /meet

6 throughout /we /behind /project /the /schedule /were

3 Complete the sentences with the correct form (present perfect or past simple) of the verbs in brackets.

The Economist

Business

Cause for scandal?

Executive pay

In August Pierre Bilger, a former Chief Executive of Alstom, (^{1} decide) ___*decided*___ to hand back the $4.1m severance package granted to him in March when he (^{2} step) _____ down from the troubled French engineering group. He said he (^{3} not /want) _____ to be cause for scandal among the 100,000 Alstom employees he (^{4} direct) _____ before the company was rescued by the French government.

Mr Bilger's example (^{5} be /not /yet) _____ followed by his compatriot Jean-Marie Messier, the former boss of Vivendi Universal. Mr Messier is still fighting to keep the €20.5m severance package due to him after the company (^{6} sack) _____ him.

Yet golden parachutes and severance pay are only one part of executive compensation. Share options (^{7} already /come) _____ under close investigation. The amounts which companies (^{8} award) _____ through share options in recent years are far higher than those paid out by golden parachutes or by any other mechanism. Even in 2001, after the stockmarket bubble (^{9} burst) _____, the value of stock options granted to the CEOs of the companies on Standard & Poor's 500 Stock Index (^{10} rise) _____ by 43.6% in a year when the total returns from those companies (^{11} fall) _____ by almost 12%.

Stock options (^{12} lead to) _____ angry reactions from both shareholders and the general public. Last year, for example, Jeffrey Barbakow, the Chief Executive of Tenet Healthcare, a hospital management business in California, (^{13} receive) _____ $111m from exercising his stock options in a year when the company's share price (^{14} drop) _____ by nearly 60%. After a group of shareholders led by a Florida doctor (^{15} threaten) _____ to remove him, Mr Barbakow (^{16} resign) _____ last May

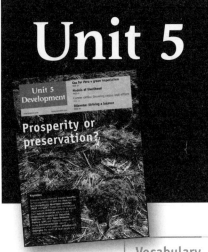

Unit 5 Development

Unit 5
Development

Prosperity or
preservation?

Vocabulary: **Development**
Language: **Modals of likelihood**
Career skills: **Predicting consequences**
Writing: **Email requesting information**

Vocabulary

1 Which word is the odd one out in each set?

	a	b	c	d
1	a <u>contract</u>	b talk	c speech	d presentation
2	a fuel	b gas	c oil	d pipeline
3	a body	b organisation	c company	d species
4	a disfigure	b damage	c protect	d endanger
5	a reduce	b release	c cut	d minimise
6	a resource	b plant	c site	d location

2 Match the pairs.

1 natural   a development
2 electricity   b resources
3 access   c fuel
4 sustainable   d how
5 fossil   e owner
6 know   f road
7 land   g forest
8 rain   h supply

3 Match the sentence halves.

1 To help fight poverty, we want to cancel   b
2 We now know we have to face
3 Governments should impose
4 We are aiming to award
5 The government has agreed to take
6 Environmentalists are making an

a the contract to a local company.
b the debt of many poor countries.
c attempt to stop the project.
d fines on companies that cause damage.
e uncomfortable facts about the environment.
f a number of precautions.

1 **Listen to a presentation about a development organisation and answer the questions.**

1 Which organisation is mentioned?   *World Bank*
2 Who does it work with?
3 Where does it operate?
4 What are its aims?

2 **Now complete the sentences to make a presentation about the same subject. Listen again if necessary.**

1 Thank you very much for inviting me to make this presentation about ...   *The World Bank*
2 As I'm sure many of you already know, ...
3 We co-operate with ...
4 We work on ...
5 Basically, we aim to ...
5 For example, we ...

3 **The following words from the presentation have the same noun and verb form. Is the pronunciation of the noun and verb form the same or different? Underline the stressed syllable.**
same
loan   access   project   aim   challenge

Read about another development organisation, the OECD. In some lines there is an extra word. Underline the incorrect word or write CORRECT next to the line number.

CORRECT	0	The Organisation for Economic Cooperation and
	1	Development (OECD) was established for to help
	2	countries develop their economies after a World War
	3	II. It as soon became a meeting place or forum for the
	4	governments of the more than economically
	5	developed countries of the world to discuss about,
	6	compare and improve their economic and social
	7	policies. As an international organisation, OECD is
	8	funded by contributions and from member country
	9	governments. In the return, OECD provides
	10	them advice, statistics and data on a wide range of subjects.

1 Complete the sentences about environmental consequences with *in, of, on, to* or *by*.

1 Delays have been caused ____*by*____ extended investigations into the route of the pipeline.

2 We're concerned that this development will result _____ environmental damage.

3 Due _____ lobbying by environmentalists, the construction project has been cancelled.

4 The involvement of too many groups might have a negative effect _____ our progress.

5 The protesters hope that their example will lead _____ similar action by other people.

6 A number of jobs have been created as a result _____ investment in this project.

7 The improvement in our standard of living has had a massive impact _____ the environment.

8 We're hoping government action will mean improvements _____ working conditions.

2 The following modal verbs are used to talk about future likelihood. Put the verbs in the correct groups.

will   may   should   is going to   might   would   could   must

certainty	probability	possibility
will		

1 Before you listen to a business news report, put the following countries in the correct groups.

USA Brazil Russia Germany Canada Italy China France Japan Britain India

BRIC	G7
Brazil	*USA*
Russia	*Germany*

2 Now listen and check your answers.

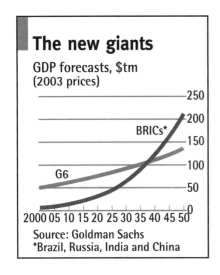

The new giants

GDP forecasts, $tm
(2003 prices)

Source: Goldman Sachs
*Brazil, Russia, India and China

3 Listen again. Are the predictions *true* or *false*?

1 The Chinese economy could soon be bigger than the economy of each G7 country.   *true*

2 The economies of the BRIC countries will soon start to slow down.

3 Germany may become the only western country with a major economy.

4 India's economy might become larger than Japan's within 30 years.

4 Look at the audioscript on page 82 and underline the verb forms used to refer to future likelihood.

5 Match the pairs. Then look at the audioscript again and check your answers.

1 currency   a economy
2 population   b movement
3 political   c forccast
4 emerging   d growth
5 long-term   e instability

Writing **1** Write five predictions about a country you know using a different verb form for each.

1 *Unemployment in the UK should remain low this year.*

2 _____

3 _____

4 _____

5 _____

2 Complete the job advertisement with the following words.

advice poverty revenue data roads supplies know-how damage

Helix International, a charitable organisation set up to reduce 1 _poverty_ in the developing world, is running a number of projects in Latin America. These include building access 2_____, introducing electricity 3_____, and eliminating soil 4_____.

We are currently looking for consultants to bring their 5_____ to our organisation. If you have experience of the following, get in touch with us: analysing 6_____, providing economic 7_____ to clients, generating 8_____.

Contact **vacancies@helix.co.uk** for an information pack giving details about these roles.

3 Now write an email (40–60 words including contact details) in response to the Helix job advertisement:

– referring to where you saw the advert
– requesting an application pack
– telling them where to send the pack.

Then compare your answer with the suggested answer on page 93.

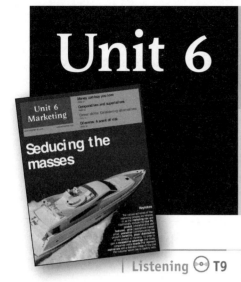

Unit 6 Marketing

Unit 6
Marketing

Seducing the masses

Vocabulary: **Marketing**
Language: **Comparatives and superlatives**
Career skills: **Considering alternatives**
Writing: **Email comparing candidates**

Listening ⊙ T9

1 Listen to a news report about price differences in Europe and answer the questions.

1 Give two facts about the DKW price survey.   *Covers 6 euro countries.*
2 Name ten items mentioned in the report.
3 Give three reasons for the price variations across Europe.

2 Listen again. Are the statements *true* or *false*?

1 Nurofen tablets are more expensive in Rome than Amsterdam.   *true*
2 Price gaps have become narrower across Europe in the last two years.
3 Madrid isn't as expensive a city as Paris.
4 All products are dearer in Brussels than in other European cities.
5 Electrical goods have the largest price differences in Europe.
6 Tax is one of the most important influences on prices in Europe.
7 Price differences in America are the same as those in Europe.
8 London is no longer the most expensive city in Europe.

Language check

Read the article about marketing in Scandinavia. Complete the article with the following words.

happiest   than   least   best   equal   most   generous   more

A midsummer night's dream

In the world of marketing, images of the Nordic states are often used to suggest healthy, honest lifestyles, but how does the image compare to the reality? Well, to be a citizen of one of these countries today is to be ¹ *more* assured of wealth, political stability, generous welfare, low crime and a good life ² _____ in most other countries. In international comparisons, one of the Nordic five (Norway, Sweden, Denmark, Finland and Iceland) is regularly at the top. Finns are the ³ _____ corrupt people anywhere. Norwegians enjoy the ⁴ _____ standard of living. The Finnish economy is the ⁵ _____ competitive after America. The Nordics as a group are the ⁶ _____ in their jobs, and most ⁷ _____ with foreign aid. Nordic women enjoy more ⁸ _____ treatment with men than those anywhere else – and so on.

1 **Which of the verbs does not match each noun?**

1 A PRODUCT
   a influence   b design   c sell   d advertise

2 A BRAND
   a establish   b create   c build   d open

3 A MARKET
   a target   b dominate   c guarantee   d enter

4 AN IMAGE
   a distribute   b have   c project   d present

5 AWARENESS
   a raise   b heighten   c pick up   d increase

2 **Complete the sentences with the correct options a–c.**

1 Younger customers regularly ___*c*___ from one brand to another.
   a branch   b distract   c switch

2 It's crucial to _____ up a good client base.
   a extend   b build   c increase

3 Our competitors are trying to _____ us from expanding.
   a destroy   b disappoint   c deter

4 The logo stands _____ quality and value for money.
   a for   b out   c in

5 Consumers _____ the product with glamour and social status.
   a aspire   b associate   c attach

6 Our aim is to _____ up with a new concept.
   a come   b go   c take

7 The Mani perfume range _____ to the younger end of the market.
   a attracts   b advertises   c appeals

8 The market has changed beyond _____ .
   a recognition   b proportion   c expectation

3 **Complete the sentences with *into*, *with*, *to*, *of*, *up* or *on*.**

1 My colleague always comes up __*with*__ such good ideas.
2 What is your attitude _____ brands?
3 Consumers can be manipulated _____ buying things.
4 We need to focus _____ our new marketing campaign.
5 We need to appeal _____ a wider range of consumers.
6 They are accused _____ copying a rival's advertising strategy.
7 New markets are opening _____ all the time.
8 People are spending more _____ beauty products than before.

4 Complete the table below.

	adjective	noun
1	guilty	*guilt*
2		consistency
3	ambitious	
4		reliability
5		competition
6		responsibility
7	secure	
8		cynicism
9	evil	
10		value

Writing

1 Complete the job advertisement with the correct form of the words in brackets.

Marketing Manager

JTC is one of the country's most established (^{1}distribute) *distribution* companies. We are currently looking for a highly-motivated and experienced Marketing Manager to join our (.organise) _____. The (^{3}succeed) _____ candidate will lead a team of more than 50 staff throughout the region. We expect you to have a professional (^{4}qualify) _____ and experience of brand management, market (^{5}analyse) _____ , (^{6}advertise) _____ and communications. You will also be (^{7}create) _____ and willing to take responsibility for (^{8}extend) _____ our current market.

Interested? Click here for details about how to apply.

2 You have interviewed two candidates for the Marketing Manager position advertised above. Write a brief email to a colleague:

- letting him /her know who you want to offer the position to and why
- including a comparison of the candidates' qualifications and experience
- comparing the salary hoped for by the candidate(s) with the salary offered
- making a general comment about the successful candidate.

Then compare your answer with the suggested answer on page 93.

1 Read the article and answer the questions.

1 Name the promotional Economist campaign of the 1980s mentioned in the article.   *White out of Red*

2 What was the result of the campaign?

3 Give an example of a successful slogan from the campaign.

Well written, and red

The Economist brand was the subject of a talk organised by the recently formed Isle of Man group of The Chartered Institute of Marketing. The talk was the second event for the Institute in the Island, and was sponsored by Mainstream Media in association with The Economist.

Titled "Well written and Red", the talk was 1 *given* by Robin Riddle, The Economist's northern UK Sales and Marketing Manager with particular responsibility for the magazine's commercial 2_____ in the Isle of Man and the Channel Islands.

His presentation outlined the success of the magazine's "White out of Red" promotional 3_____ launched in the 1980s, which had resulted in growth in its 4_____ base, and heightened global brand 5_____, both of which, he said, had been achieved without discounting the product.

The success of the campaign, which had seen The Economist's 6_____ revenue grow by 250 per cent since 1987, could, said Mr Riddle, serve as an inspiration to other businesses, helping them to 7_____ hard decisions.

Despite these difficult decisions, said Mr Riddle, the late eighties had enabled the company to 8_____ its product more effectively and so target its 9_____ more easily.

Mr Riddle said that The Economist's independence was the key to its success. The Economist is now on sale in 200 countries and enjoys a UK circulation matching that of the Financial Times. Choosing to 10_____ a unique position on global events and combining unexpected views with clever comments had contributed to this success.

With a modest advertising budget, The Economist had succeeded in keeping and finding customers through an innovative campaign based on the concept of "what it would do for you." Posters in the magazine's distinctive red and white colours caught the spirit of the late eighties and nineties, with award winning advertisements such as "If your assistant reads The Economist, don't play too much golf" and "Given a choice, would you pick your brain?"

In opinion polls, 100% of Economist readers had one. *The Economist*

2 Match the pairs then use them to complete the article.

1	target	a	a position
2	give	b	a market
3	adopt	c	a talk
4	make	d	a product
5	position	e	a decision
6	advertising	f	base
7	client	g	revenue
8	brand	h	interests
9	promotional	i	awareness
10	commercial	j	campaign

Unit 7 Outsourcing

Vocabulary: Outsourcing
Language: Conditionals 1 and 2
Career skills: Making and responding to suggestions
Writing: Email requesting suggestions

Vocabulary

1 **Match the words with the definitions.**

1	offshoring	**a**	amount more than is needed
2	call centre	**b**	transfer of operations to lower cost countries
3	surplus	**c**	routine administrative tasks
4	outsourcing	**d**	regular costs of running a business (e.g. rent, heating)
5	trade union	**e**	amount which is not enough
6	shortage	**f**	central office dealing with large numbers of phone calls
7	overheads	**g**	buying from outside suppliers
8	back-office jobs	**h**	organisation that represents the interests of employees

2 **Complete the sentences with the correct options a–c.**

1 A local team should ____c____ complex customer service requests.
   a track   **b** contract   **c** handle

2 We can transfer Customer Service to outside service _____.
   a providers   **b** subsidiaries   **c** workforces

3 Businesses are trying to _____ savings through offshoring.
   a do   **b** make   **c** take

4 Simple work like _____ credit card receipts is often outsourced.
   a dealing   **b** processing   **c** controlling

5 You could _____ up a subsidiary in Eastern Europe.
   a hang   **b** put   **c** set

6 The trade unions are considering industrial _____.
   a action   **b** management   **c** behaviour

7 Will you _____ the pilot project for the offshore centre?
   a overdo   **b** overtake   **c** oversee

8 Offshoring will _____ to the improvement of company performance.
   a supply   **b** contribute   **c** transfer

9 How will _____ to sensitive areas of information be controlled?
   a business   **b** process   **c** access

10 We've had to make people redundant ito compete with a major _____.
   a challenge   **b** rival   **c** competition

1 Read the article about offshoring in India. Use the headings to make notes about the two types of companies involved.

	companies based in higher cost countries	contractors based in lower cost countries
Companies involves in offshoring	Thames Water	Wipro
Potential benefits off ofshoring to these companies	Can save 30–40%	Increase in turnover

The Economist

Business

A lift from India

How offshoring gives companies an advantage

ONE of the reasons why the trade-unionists of Amicus have nominated David Prosser (Chief Executive of life insurers Legal & General) Britain's best boss is that he has promised not to send jobs abroad. L&G's shareholders may be less happy: its rivals, and many other companies, are rushing to buy their service work offshore, to their competitive advantage.

Companies in India – by far the biggest supplier – think that business process outsourcing (BPO) may bring that country $4 billion from abroad this year, a rise of more than 50%. Over half of that will be from America, but Britain's share will be at least one-tenth, the equivalent of some 20,000 lowish-paid jobs.

Just how much companies save by offshoring work will depend on how good they are at doing it. Stelios Haji-Ioannou says his easyGroup's hire-car arm actually makes money by outsourcing customer calls, since the customer pays 60p a minute, more than his firm pays the Indian call centre. But dealing with Bangalore is not like handling the call centre down the corridor, even if the Indians concerned are your own employees.

The more usual call centre client can look to save 30–40%. For more complex offshoring, a round figure might be 25–30%: a worthwhile saving if IT, as it well may, makes up a tenth of your overall costs. But calculations of savings are imprecise, because they do not come just from low Indian wages. Like any consultants, the three big Indian companies selling these services – Wipro, Tata Consultancy Services (TCS) and slightly smaller Infosys – are offering better solutions, not just cheapness.

These are big firms: when the figures are out, their combined 2003–04 turnover will be $3.5 billion, a rise of one third. Their lists of British clients are long and well-known: Thames Water, United Utilities, Sainsbury, BT, BA, P&O, National Grid, Barclays, Prudential and others in finance, and many more. Wipro has worked for years with Thames Water; TCS is part of a consortium that has just signed up to sort out

some National Health Service IT; Infosys is to help improve a BT system for getting its staff to the right place at the right time.

British firms are much keener on offshoring than are those in other EU countries. Although the Indian consultants have offices across Europe, TCS gets nearly 20% of its work from Britain, double what it gets from the rest of Europe put together. Wipro's trade is more balanced: 12% British, around 20% from other Europeans. (But Britain is only one-sixth of the west European economy!) These figures reflect India's historic relationship with the UK: English is widely spoken and the countries share Anglo-American traditions. However, continental countries are bound to catch up. German, Dutch and Belgian firms are looking offshore. Even Ireland, once a place to go offshore to, will become a country seeking to outsource overseas like its rivals.

Everyone's a winner [1]

Benefit per $1 of US spending sent offshore, 2002 est

United States

Savings accruing to US investors/customers	0.58
Imports of US goods and services by providers in India	0.05
Transfer of profits by US-based providers in India back to US	0.04
Net direct benefit retained in US	0.67
Value from US labour re-employed	0.45–0.47
Potential net benefit to US	1.12–1.14

India

Labour	0.10
Profits retained in India	0.10
Suppliers	0.09
Central government taxes	0.03
State government taxes	0.01
Net benefit to India	0.33

Source: McKinsey Global Institute

2 Look at the article again. What do these numbers refer to?

1 $4 billion   *possible income for India this year from BPO*
2 50%
3 20,000
4 60p
5 30–40%
6 $3.5 billion
7 12%
8 1/6

3 Look at the article again. Find words with similar meanings.

1 chosen   *nominated*
2 competitor
3 overseas
4 increase
5 the same as
6 dealing with
7 inexact
8 answers
9 sales
10 business

4 Complete the table below with vocabulary about job cuts.

	adjective	verb	noun
1	cut	cut	cut
2	reduced		
3	lost		
4		make redundant	
5			layoff

5 Now complete the sentences.

1 Although offshoring creates jobs in countries with lower costs, it results in job ___cuts___ in countries with higher costs.
2 The Bank of America has experience of corporate downsizing. It has made 3,700 staff in technical and back-office jobs _____.
3 Companies should tell staff of plans resulting in _____ .
4 Governments may face a backlash in countries where massive numbers of workers have been _____ off because of offshoring.
5 Unions are becoming more active to stop further job _____ in places where jobs have been transferred overseas.
6 In order _____ unemployment at home, some states want legislation against moving jobs overseas.

Look at the suggestions and conditional sentences. Find and correct the mistakes.

brainstorming

1 What about ~~to brainstorm~~ different ways of cutting costs?
2 If we would advertise more, we would be better known.
3 We would save money if we will move our back-office work overseas.
4 If I would be you, I'd identify the major cost areas.
5 We might be better off if we will consult with the unions.
6 If we will reduce overheads, we may reach our targets.
7 If we won't get more contracts, we have to take serious steps.
8 I suggest to employ consultants to help us decide what action to take.

1 **A group of colleagues discuss outsourcing. Listen and answer the questions.**

1 What business function do they want to outsource?   *Customer Service*
2 What options do they discuss?
3 What do they decide to do?

2 **Listen again and complete the speakers' suggestions.**

1 I really think we should ...   *outsource our Customer Service division.*
2 How about ...
3 One way would be to ...
4 What if we ...
5 Let's ...
6 I suggest ...
7 Couldn't we ...

Write an email in response to Elena. Use the information from the conversation above.

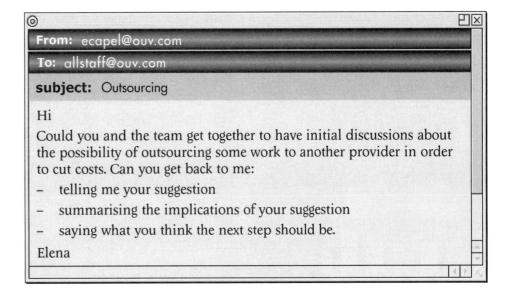

From: ecapel@ouv.com
To: allstaff@ouv.com

subject: Outsourcing

Hi
Could you and the team get together to have initial discussions about the possibility of outsourcing some work to another provider in order to cut costs. Can you get back to me:
– telling me your suggestion
– summarising the implications of your suggestion
– saying what you think the next step should be.
Elena

Then compare your answer with the suggested answer on page 93.

Unit 8
Finance

The bottom line

Vocabulary: **Finance**
Language: **Adjectives and adverbs**
Career skills: **Referring to visuals**
Writing: **Short report describing a graph**

Listening ⊙ T11

1 Put the verbs in the correct groups. Which are also nouns?

grow go down go up rise decline increase drop decrease fall
plunge plummet soar jump skyrocket nosedive slide dip

upward trend	downward trend

2 Listen to a news report. Match each country with a sentence. Then listen again and tick any of the verbs above that you hear.

1 Germany — a The rate of unemployment decreased.
2 Austria —— b Industrial production went down.
3 Switzerland   c Retail sales nosedived.
4 UK   d The economy grew.

Language check

1 In some lines there is an extra word. Underline the incorrect word or write CORRECT next to the line number.

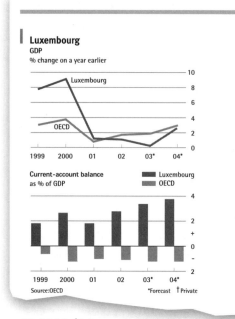

Luxembourg
GDP
% change on a year earlier

Luxembourg

OECD

1999 2000 01 02 03* 04*

Current-account balance as % of GDP   ■ Luxembourg ■ OECD

1999 2000 01 02 03* 04*
Source:OECD   *Forecast †Private

0 | Luxembourg's economy has fallen <u>down</u> dramatically since the
1 | boom years of 1999 and 2000, when economic growth has
2 | averaged 8.8%. Thanks to the banking and finance, which
3 | account for a third of GDP, Luxembourg's economy grew more
4 | faster than most others during the global economic boom. But
5 | the slowdown that followed has hit hard. The OECD now
6 | expects the country's economy to grow up by just 0.3% in 2003
7 | and by 2.7% in 2004. The slowdown will be slight worsened by
8 | Luxembourg's generous state pension benefits and such early
9 | retirements. Only a quarter of Luxembourgeois aged between 55
10 | and 64 are in work. Despite of the slowdown, Luxembourg will
   | continue to rely on foreign workers.

2 Look at the sentences with adjectives and adverbs. Find and correct the mistakes.

1 There was a ~~dramatically~~ *dramatic* jump in turnover last year.
2 Share prices have fallen very quick.
3 The company has been extreme slow to cut costs.
4 Company performance is expected to improve steady over the year.
5 Following the takeover, the future looks positively for MNP.

3 Put the words in the correct order to make presentation phrases.

1 see you as can   *as you can see*
2 that will you notice
3 the move let's on to slide next
4 clearly graph the shows
5 see the led this to trend you here has

4 Now look at a presentation about poverty in the USA. Complete the presentation using the phrases above.

Poverty and health-insurance status

People, m

As % of total population

Without health insurance — 15.2 – 45

40

Below poverty level — 12.1 – 35

30

1993 94 95 96 97 98 99 2000 01 02

Source: Census Bureau

Right, let's look at the first slide: *Poverty and health-insurance status.*
1 ___*As you can see*___ , poverty has grown worse in the USA.
2 _____ that the number of people below the poverty level has risen steadily since 2000. Also, 3 _____ the number of Americans without health insurance is soaring. In fact, now more than 12% of Americans don't have health insurance. Why is this? Well, it's generally thought that a rise in the cost of health-insurance premiums 4 _____ .

OK, 5 _____ . This shows the average household cash income, which fell for the third year running in 2002, to around $42,000. Another worrying trend.

These figures don't make good reading, but they do need to be put into context. It's important to realise that despite being higher than it was at the height of the recent economic boom – around the year 2000 – America's poverty rate is still below the average of the past two decades.

5 Look at more detailed figures about poverty in the USA. Complete the sentences with *between, in, of, from, to* or *by*.

1 The percentage of people receiving health insurance from their employers fell ___*from*___ 62.6% _____ 61.3% _____ 2002.
2 _____ 2002, the number of Americans without health insurance rose _____ 5.7% _____ 43.6m.
3 1.7m more people fell below the poverty line _____ 2000 and 2002. This meant that there was an increase _____ the poverty rate _____ 4%, _____ 11.7% _____ 12.1%.

Match the pairs.

1	sales	a	sheet
2	balance	b	revenue
3	credit	c	value
4	market	d	rating
5	insider	e	operations
6	retained	f	assets
7	foreign	g	trading
8	fixed	h	profit

1 Match the words with the definitions.

1	allegations	a	owners of a company's shares
2	irregularities	b	accusations that have not been proved
3	shareholders	c	given official approval
4	peak	d	legally responsible
5	investigation	e	business deal/arrangement
6	authorised	f	official examination of the facts
7	takeover	g	highest point
8	stock market	h	acquisition of a company
9	assets	i	where shares are bought and sold
10	liable	j	attempt
11	transaction	k	things/property a company or person owns
12	bid	l	accounting practices that do not obey the normal rules

2 Read the article below and answer the questions.

1 What is the scandal at Skandia? *irregularities by top managers*
2 What did the report by independent investigators reveal?
3 Why might Skandia now be the target of a takeover?
4 How successful was Skandia's move into the American market?
5 Does the future look positive or negative for Skandia?

Writing   Write a short description (80–100 words) describing and explaining the changes in the share price at Skandia, based on the graph. Then compare your answer with the suggested answer on page 94.

The Economist

Business

Skandal

An insurer's damaged reputation

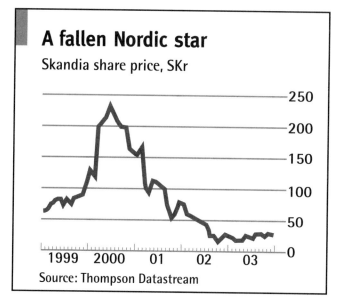

A fallen Nordic star

Skandia share price, SKr

Source: Thompson Datastream

SWEDEN is in the middle of one of its biggest corporate scandals. In the spring, there were allegations of misbehaviour by top managers at Skandia, the country's biggest insurer. On December 1st a report by independent investigators outlined the extent of 'irregularities'. The company's chairman, Bengt Braun, resigned. Though not accused of doing wrong, Mr Braun had been on the board when some executives made themselves rich at shareholders' expense.

The findings of the 156-page report by Otto Rydbeck, a lawyer, and Goran Tidstrom, an accountant, are shocking.

Executives told shareholders that they received SKr356m ($37m) in bonus payments between 2000 and 2002, but in fact took home a further SKr550m. In 1997 and 1998 Skandia had launched two bonus programmes, both with limits authorised by the board of directors, explains Mr Rydbeck. But former chief executive Lars-Eric Petersson himself removed the limit on the second scheme in October 2000. "Mr Petersson should be personally liable for the SKr550m," says Mr Rydbeck.

Stockholm's public prosecutor is launching a criminal investigation into this payment and another transaction from which Mr Petersson and his deputy, Ulf Spang, received SKr70m more than authorised. Mr Petersson, Mr Spang and Ola Ramstedt, the head of Skandia's life-insurance business, took corporate flats for themselves and their relatives. The flats were renovated at the company's expense.

The scandal is doing the insurer's financial health no good at all. Skandia's share price is one-tenth of its peak in June 2000. On December 2nd Sampo, a Finnish company and Skandia's biggest shareholder, denied that it was planning a takeover bid.

Once Skandia was a favourite of growth investors. In the 1990s it successfully entered the American market. But the stockmarket crash showed how much Skandia was affected by stockmarket changes. It started making operating losses and in December 2002 Skandia was forced to sell American Skandia to Prudential Financial, an American insurer.

Even so, say analysts, Skandia is basically a healthy company: the bad old bosses have gone and their successors are bringing in changes to improve the business.

Unit 9 Recruitment

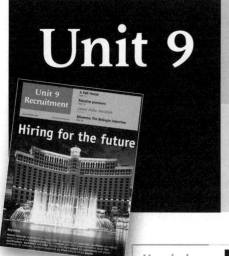

Unit 9 Recruitment

Hiring for the future

Vocabulary: **Recruitment**
Language: **Relative pronouns**
Career skills: **Small talk**
Writing: **Email applying for a job**

Vocabulary

1 How many nouns related to recruitment can you find in the word search?

c	t	*g*	*r*	*a*	*d*	*u*	*a*	*t*	*e*
a	c	c	e	p	t	a	n	c	e
n	t	m	e	s	e	r	s	h	m
d	a	n	c	y	s	a	e	e	s
i	o	f	f	e	r	t	l	c	c
d	z	x	b	n	m	i	e	k	r
a	d	v	e	r	t	n	c	s	e
t	t	h	i	r	e	g	t	a	e
e	t	p	o	s	i	t	i	o	n
k	i	n	t	e	r	v	i	e	w

2 Which of the verbs does not match each noun?

1 A SITUATION
   a handle   **b** approach   **c** <u>operate</u>   **d** deal with   **e** experience
2 AN APPLICANT
   a select   **b** retire   **c** screen   **d** evaluate   **e** reject
3 AN INTERVIEW
   a carry out   **b** attend   **c** conduct   **d** hold   **e** make
4 AN EMPLOYEE
   a hire   **b** implement   **c** fire   **d** recruit   **e** appoint
5 A DEADLINE
   a take   **b** fix   **c** meet   **d** set   **e** miss
6 A JOB
   a accept   **b** leave   **c** offer   **d** regulate   **e** apply for

3 Match the pairs.

1 back   a talk
2 time   b ground
3 small   c limit
4 pay   d base
5 cover   e roll
6 data   f letter

4 Now use the word pairs to complete the sentences.

1 A _time limit_ was set: recruiters would interview 60 people in four days.
2 Applicants were asked to send in an online CV with a _____.
3 Interviewers asked questions about each candidate's _____.
4 Applicants demonstrated communication skills by engaging in _____.
5 The applicants' scores were fed into a _____.
6 To speed things up, the same technology was used to process both HR and _____ forms.

5 Complete the sentences with *to*, *for*, *from* or *in*.

1 I am thinking of applying __for__ the position of Team Leader.
2 We are looking for people with a degree _____ pharmacology.
3 Peter is responsible _____ over 100 members of staff.
4 The latest recruit graduated _____ university only last year.
5 Sergio has been assigned _____ this branch since Paula left.
6 Who will be accountable _____ the quality of all our work?

6 Complete the table below.

	verb	noun
1	interview	*interview*
2	require	
3		qualification
4	advertise	
5		selection
6		notification
7	apply	
8	recruit	
9		specification
10	accept	

1 Underline the correct relative pronouns in italics. Then identify the sentences where it is possible to delete the relative pronoun.

1 Thank you for your CV, <u>which</u> / that I received yesterday.

2 Maggie Night is the person whose / whom application form has gone missing.

3 Howard Carey, who / what is our HR manager, will be in touch shortly.

4 I am attaching the form that / who you need to complete.

5 The applicants that / what are successful will hear within two weeks.

6 Jeremy, who / that has worked here for three years, has just resigned.

7 The cover letters which / who I have received are in my office.

8 The person to whom / whose you need to speak is called Graham.

2 Put the words in the correct order to make useful phrases for small talk.

1 you /what /sorry /did /say?   *Sorry, what did you say?*

2 be /I'd /I /guess /better /going

3 me /you /would /excuse?

4 you /meeting /nice

5 want /to /I /don't /you /keep /any /longer

6 don't /why /you /give /a /call /me?

7 to /great /you /talking

8 you /some /time /soon /see

9 exactly /what /mean /do /that /you /by?

10 didn't /realise /was /I /it /late /so

1 Put the sentences in the correct order to make a telephone conversation. Then listen to check your answers.

a Really! ☐

b Yeah, but didn't they think it was strange? ☐

c I know, I can hardly believe it myself, especially as I sent the application form to the wrong address! ☐

d Err ... I don't think so. I just told them the original form was ripped, and they sent me a new one straight away. Oh, is that the time? I'm sorry, but I really have to go. I've got to make a quick call about the job. Anyway, why don't you ring me and maybe we could have lunch some time? ☐

e You're kidding! How could you do a thing like that? ☐

f Sure. Good luck with the interview, by the way. ☐

g Hi Anne, Martin here. I just wanted to let you know I've got an interview for the management job I applied for with CTD. 1

h I was addressing the envelope in a hurry and got mixed up. Luckily, I realised what I'd done and so I just rang up and asked the company for another form. ☐

i Thanks, bye. ☐

2 Now look at the audioscript on page 84 and underline any useful words and phrases for small talk.

1 Your friend sends you an email with an attached job advertisement. You decide to apply for the job. Use your notes to write a cover letter to send with your CV.

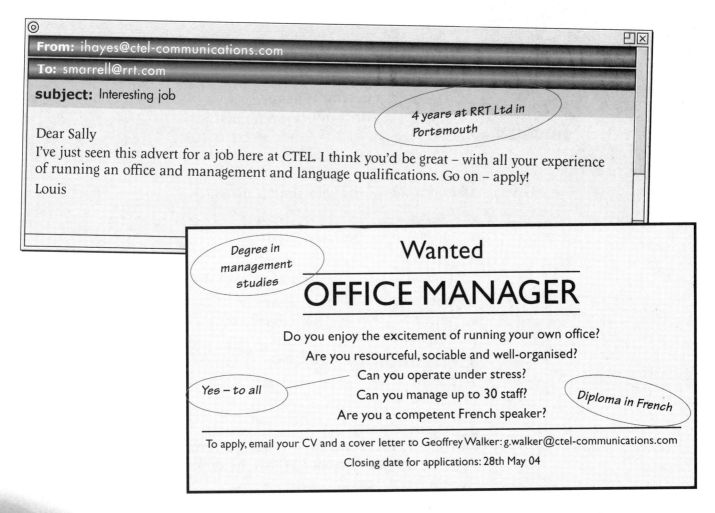

From: ihayes@ctel-communications.com
To: smarrell@rrt.com
subject: Interesting job

4 years at RRT Ltd in Portsmouth

Dear Sally

I've just seen this advert for a job here at CTEL. I think you'd be great – with all your experience of running an office and management and language qualifications. Go on – apply!

Louis

Degree in management studies

Wanted
OFFICE MANAGER

Do you enjoy the excitement of running your own office?
Are you resourceful, sociable and well-organised?
Can you operate under stress?
Can you manage up to 30 staff?
Are you a competent French speaker?

Yes – to all

Diploma in French

To apply, email your CV and a cover letter to Geoffrey Walker: g.walker@ctel-communications.com
Closing date for applications: 28th May 04

2 Read a letter applying for the job. Find and correct any mistakes.

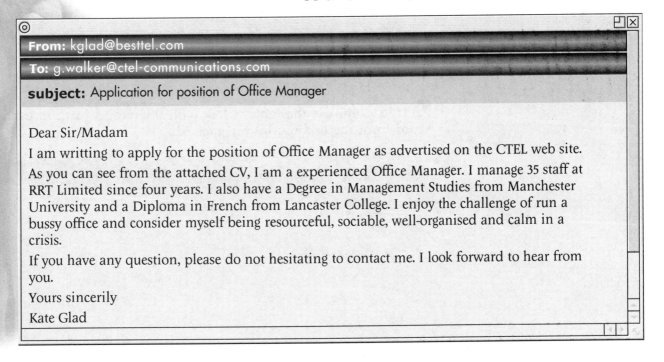

From: kglad@besttel.com
To: g.walker@ctel-communications.com
subject: Application for position of Office Manager

Dear Sir/Madam

I am writting to apply for the position of Office Manager as advertised on the CTEL web site.

As you can see from the attached CV, I am a experienced Office Manager. I manage 35 staff at RRT Limited since four years. I also have a Degree in Management Studies from Manchester University and a Diploma in French from Lancaster College. I enjoy the challenge of run a bussy office and consider myself being resourceful, sociable, well-organised and calm in a crisis.

If you have any question, please do not hesitating to contact me. I look forward to hear from you.

Yours sincerily

Kate Glad

Unit 10 Counterfeiting

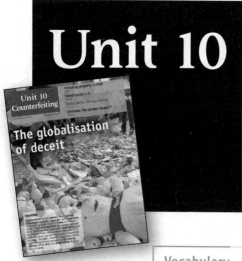

Unit 10 Counterfeiting

The globalisation of deceit

Vocabulary: Counterfeiting
Language: Conditionals 1–3
Career skills: Giving reasons
Writing: Note giving reasons

Vocabulary

1 Match the words with similar meanings.

1	legitimate	a	exchange
2	counterfeit	b	legal
3	covert	c	brand
4	genuine	d	indistinguishable
5	trademark	e	fake
6	imitate	f	breach
7	identical	g	real
8	swap	h	copy
9	peer	i	secret
10	infringement	j	equal

Listening T13

1 Listen to an extract from a radio programme. Which companies does the speaker mention? Which are online music services?

2 Listen again. Are the statements *true* or *false*?

1 Record companies formed alliances to develop distribution. *true*
2 Warner Brothers and EMI merged in 2000.
3 Sales of recorded music decreased in 2001 but started to rise in 2002.
4 Napster is one of the smallest online file swapping services.
5 iTunes, a pay service, has done well.

3 Now complete the table below with the correct form of each word from the audioscript on page 84.

	verb	noun
1	*copy*	copy
2	acquire	
3	entertain	
4		replacement
5	sell	
6		merger

The Economist

Music

Upbeat

Is the threat of online piracy disappearing?

WHY is peer-to-peer sharing (where people download music from the internet and then share it with friends rather than buying singles or albums from large recording companies) so popular? The fact that peer-to-peer sharing is free will always be appealing. On the other hand, paying 99 cents for a song on iTunes (a pay online music service) is unappealing, says one British teen, because at that price she may as well buy the CD in a shop. Nor do the new services match the libraries of nearly all music ever recorded that the peer-to-peers claim to have.

As for the risk of a lawsuit from the Recording Industry Association of America (RIAA), the selling point for new versions of peer-to-peer networks in recent months is that they can protect the identity of users. The most popular of the range now is Earth Station 5, which is based in the Jenin refugee camp on the West Bank. After the RIAA said it would take legal action, its software was downloaded more than 16m times in 90 hours. So far, it seems to work.

Looking towards the future, big music companies should look not at iTunes' encouraging figures but at September's price cut by Universal Music Group (UMG), the biggest record company of all, which reduced the cost of its CDs for consumers by nearly a quarter. One reason for falling music sales is that customers believe that CDs cost too much. Now, other firms will have to lower prices to compete with Universal. Discount stores such as Wal-Mart, Circuit City and Best Buy will drive them down more.

The success of iTunes has shown the music industry that many people want to buy single tracks, not albums. Apple's data show that its customers bought 12 singles for every one album at iTunes. That compares with 0.02 singles per album in American stores, according to research by Sanford Bernstein. The best artists may tempt people to buy a whole album. But the industry can no longer rely on getting the price of an album as a reward for supporting a band.

In the end, says Moby, an influential musician, the record industry will have to throw out its current business model. It will no longer be able to make huge profit margins on CDs that cost next to nothing to manufacture. To make up for lower prices, he says, the industry needs to cut its marketing for artists by as much as four-fifths. Once the record companies have less marketing influence, and with opportunities for internet distribution, says Moby, artists will be in a powerful position.

1 What does the article say about peer-to-peer sharing?
   a It has become less popular with teenagers lately.
   b It will continue to attract new users.
   c It only involves a few types of music.

2 The latest networks
   a are only for users in the Middle East.
   b have had software problems.
   c do not reveal who the user is.

3 UMG has recently
   a cut its CD prices.
   b gained new types of customer.
   c taken over a major discount store.

4 A key fact about the music industry is that
   a there is more interest in singles than albums.
   b fewer songs are put on an album than before.
   c musicians want to continue making albums.

5 Moby says that the record industry should
   a increase its profit margin.
   b cut back on its manufacturing costs.
   c reduce the amount it spends on marketing.

Language check Look at the conditional sentences. Find and correct the mistakes.

1 If they ~~would have~~ told me the that watch was fake, I wouldn't have
   bought it. *they'd told*

2 If you'll continue to sell counterfeit goods, the police will arrest you.

3 If I'd had more money, I wouldn't have bought a fake watch.

4 We will have to deal with counterfeiters if we want to succeed.

5 If we stopped counterfeiting, more foreigners will visit our country.

6 If I am you, I will take the counterfeiters to court.

7 I hadn't reported the counterfeiters to the authorities if I'd known they
   were so poor.

8 I think that the company won't be so vulnerable to counterfeiters if it
   lowers its prices.

Listening ⊙ T14

1 Jenny calls a colleague about a meeting. Listen and answer the
questions.

1 What is the purpose of her call? *to inform Max she might be late for the*
   team meeting

2 What is the outcome?

3 What does she offer to do?

2 Listen again. What words and phrases do the speakers use to
give reasons? Can you add any more?

3 Now complete the sentences appropriately.

1 I need a day off work in order ...

2 It's difficult to know what to do first, given ...

3 The reason I want to go to Rome is ...

4 The project has been delayed due ...

5 As I've got some free time, ...

Writing You need to leave the office briefly. Write a note (30–40 words) for
your colleague saying where you are going and why. Then compare
your answer with the suggested answer on page 95.

1 Read the article quickly and choose the most appropriate title.

Holidays in Asia
Computer software
How to win in court

Training customs officials
Fighting counterfeit products

The Economist

THE Tet festival marking the lunar new year, which began on February 1st, is Vietnam's most celebrated holiday, a time to go shopping. This year the government used the occasion to remind the Vietnamese that counterfeit goods are (¹lagelli) *illegal* . So avoid the (²faek) _____ designer handbags and computer software, however tempting the prices. Western companies, for long the (³cvitims) _____ of counterfeiting, welcomed the warning, as they have welcomed such warnings in the past. But they know they will continue to face a struggle when (⁴efnrocign) _____ their intellectual property rights.

Take Vietnam's customs (⁵wal) _____, passed in December 2001, which allows customs offices to hold suspected counterfeit (⁶doogs) _____ at the border, and thus stop them being exported. Under the law a company that believes its goods have been (⁷cpodie) _____ can instruct its (⁸lagel) _____

representatives to make a complaint. But the representatives are not allowed to inspect any products; that is the job of customs officials, who have to be satisfied that a reasonable case has been made.

In practice, companies simply cannot move fast enough to stop the pirated, and often (⁹sohddy) _____, products from going abroad. Not one of the foreign companies doing business in Vietnam has taken advantage of this law to prosecute those (¹⁰gifingnirn) _____ trademark rights. The problems are not confined to (¹¹namufactderu) _____ products. It is estimated that 99% of computer (¹²waretsof) _____ available in Vietnam is pirated. The companies which are (¹³ffeacted) _____ are defeatist about seeking the protection of the (¹⁴struoc). This defeatism is deepened by visits to government offices that use (¹⁵ripate) copies of Microsoft 'Office'.

2 Now put the letters in brackets in the correct order to make words from the unit.

Unit 11 Markets

Vocabulary: Markets
Language: Gerunds and infinitives
Career skills: Making offers
Writing: Email arranging a meeting

Vocabulary

1 Match the words with similar meanings.

1	trade	a	monitor
2	rival	b	exchange
3	simple	c	risk
4	threat	d	traditional
5	conventional	e	special
6	observe	f	competitor
7	unique	g	objective
8	goal	h	easy

2 Complete the table below.

	verb	noun
1	negotiate	negotiation
2	advertise	
3		auction
4	supply	
5		demand
6	discuss	

3 Which is the odd one out in each set?

	a	b	c	d
1	seller	buyer	retailer	shopkeeper
2	stock	supplies	inventory	commerce
3	outlet	auction	transaction	market
4	modify	tailor	bid	personalise
5	customer	client	consumer	commodity
6	rate	fluctuate	evaluate	grade
7	track	discover	trace	follow
8	leave	exit	withdraw	access

1 Read the article about eBay. Are the statements _true_ or _false_?

1 eBay is regarded as the top online auction company. _true_
2 The company buys goods and holds them before reselling them.
3 It makes a large profit on every deal.
4 eBay has only just started to make a profit.
5 eBay has recently bought a payments business.
6 The US Department of Justice has tried to stop eBay trading.

The Economist

Business

Breaking into new markets

A business model for e-commerce?

E Bay, the world's leading online auctioneer, has a business
¹ ___model___ that definitely suits the internet. Thanks
to many clever search features, it can match up sellers and
² _____ of even the most unfamiliar items. And
because of its smart cost and revenue structure (it charges a
modest commission on each ³ _____ and does not
store goods), eBay has been one of the most consistently
profitable e-commerce businesses. In the first quarter, its net
⁴ _____ more than doubled, to $104.2m,
on revenues of $476m. This was partly due to eBay's
⁵ _____ of PayPal, a payments business, last year.

Taking out the effects of that deal, ⁶ _____ were up by
56% over the previous year. One of eBay's greatest strengths,
however, is also one of the biggest ⁷ _____ it faces. Its
business, like any marketplace, is a natural
⁸ _____, and so once it is established, it is pretty hard
for a newcomer to challenge it. This has already aroused the
⁹ _____ of America's Department of Justice. It took no
action after an ¹⁰ _____ a couple of years ago, but
some think it will be tempted to take another look as eBay
expands.

---

2 Now complete the article with the following words.

acquisition   model   transaction   buyers   sales   income
risks   monopoly   investigation   interest

Underline the correct forms (gerund or infinitive) in italics.

1 We need to be good at _innovating_/to innovate to retain customers.
2 They advised the company _setting_/to set up an online auction.
3 Can we meet in order _speaking_/to speak about distribution?
4 It's essential _investing_/to invest in new operations.
5 We can't risk _ignoring_/to ignore this share tip.
6 I suggest _evaluating_/to evaluate our website immediately.
7 _Building_/To build up long-term relationships isn't easy.
8 Have you decided _taking over_/to take over another business?
9 I've managed _negotiating_/to negotiate a better deal!
10 The product is so popular that it's difficult _meeting_/to meet demand.

1 Read five extracts from an article about services and e-commerce and look at the sentences below. Which extract does each sentence refer to? Match each sentence with one of the extracts.

a

E-commerce used to be just about buying products. But now firms everywhere have launched electronic marketplaces for services of all sorts – from gardening advice to financial planning. If services now exist in the online world, those markets will become more competitive – as they have for computers and other items sold over the internet.

b

In the 1980s, the late Phil Salin dreamed up the American Information Exchange, a marketplace for research, consulting and computer code. But it never really became successful, largely because it came before the internet: much of the cash and effort went into trying to create a network.

c

Advoco, one of the few services markets that is already online, employs experts who want to give advice. Users then choose one of the 'advisers' directly or post a question on a bulletin board that they can answer with a bid. Once the service is delivered and paid for, users rate the sellers on a scale from one (lowest) to five (highest) and post comments about them.

d

Supply of labour is not likely to be a problem for service sites. Some companies already have hundreds of professionals, attracted by word of mouth alone. Joining is free – and more promising than an expensive ad. What is more, for professionals living in developing countries, these online forums offer a unique opportunity to enter richer service markets.

e

Whether there is enough demand for service sites is questionable. Small businesses and independent professionals, always short of time, might be interested. But to be widely successful, internet service markets have to overcome cultural barriers. Individuals are used to getting advice free over the internet, and will hesitate to employ a service provider whom they have never met face-to-face.

1 Early attempts at trading services electronically failed. *b*
2 Companies are sometimes graded on the service they have provided. ☐
3 It is easy to find service providers through e-commerce. ☐
4 Customers do not always expect to pay for online services. ☐
5 Services as well as goods can be bought online. ☐
6 The buying of services online can be similar to an auction. ☐
7 The winners are likely to be service providers in poorer regions. ☐

2 Match the verbs with the nouns from the extracts.

1	offer	a	a service
2	enter	b	an opportunity
3	post	c	advice
4	give	d	a market
5	overcome	e	a comment
6	provide	f	a barrier

1 Jason, a Sales Manager, talks to his colleague Molly about an online sales promotion. Listen and complete the notes.

Meeting Friday 3rd March

Participants: Sales team
Purpose: To discuss the promotion of the new (1) ... perfume

Notes:
Ask Peter for some (2) ...
Call Sally from the (3) ...
Decide whether to offer an (4) ...

2 Listen again. What phrases do the speakers use to make and respond to suggestions? Can you add any more phrases?

making suggestions	responding to suggestions
I was thinking we should ...	Good idea

Writing Write the email (60–80 words) from Molly to the sales team, giving the proposed date, time and location of the meeting about the online promotion. Explain that the meeting will cover the following:

- how best to attract customers
- promotional offers
- encouraging repeat visits to the website.

Then compare your answer with the suggested answer on page 95.

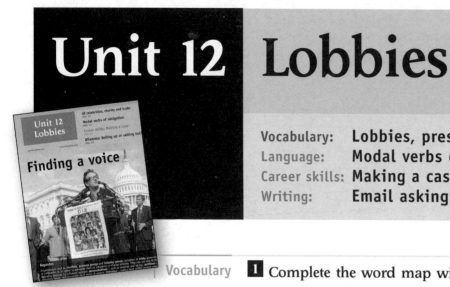

Unit 12 Lobbies

Vocabulary:	**Lobbies, pressure groups and campaigns**
Language:	**Modal verbs of obligation**
Career skills:	**Making a case**
Writing:	**Email asking for support**

Vocabulary

1 Complete the word map with the following words.

litigation   debt relief   lobby group   boycott   duty   aid   sit-in
activist   imports   campaigner   demonstration   environment
NGO   subsidies   petition   quotas   fair trade   celebrity   march
pressure group   letter of protest   tariff barriers

people and organisations
lobby group
_____
_____
_____
_____

issues
debt relief
_____
_____
_____
_____
_____
_____

lobbies

action
litigation
_____
_____
_____
_____
_____

2 Complete the sentences with *of, at, in, against, to* or *with*.

1 I think we need to take a fresh look ____*at*____ the issue of foreign aid.
2 Many people are still unaware _____ the exploitation of children.
3 The company has been bombarded _____ protests.
4 We're planning a demonstration _____ the new nuclear plant.
5 Some countries receive millions of dollars each year _____ aid.
6 The boycott was a waste _____ time.
7 We need to draw attention _____ poverty in this country.
8 Debt relief should be _____ the top of their agenda.

3 Which is the odd one out in each set?

1 a organisation   b firm   c <u>slum</u>   d institution
2 a influence   b persuade   c target   d convince
3 a rise   b condemn   c develop   d increase
4 a issue   b dilemma   c sacrifice   d problem
5 a demand   b recognise   c understand d realise
6 a regulation   b law   c pressure   d policy
7 a charity   b celebrity   c cause   d campaign
8 a cut   b exploit   c drop   d cancel

4 Match each of the following verbs with one set of nouns.

make give generate do take raise

1 ___*give*___   a grant
                   a loan
2 _____   publicity
                   interest
3 _____   action
                   part
4 _____   a difference
                   a claim
5 _____   awareness
                   funds
6 _____   good
                   harm

Language check **Underline the correct modal verbs in italics.**

1 In some places people <u>*have to*</u>/*should* work more than 12 hours a day.
2 You *mustn't*/*don't have* to donate any money if you don't want to.
3 Employers *ought to*/*must* stop using child labour or face a fine.
4 You *needn't*/*shouldn't* speak to the press. I can do it if you're busy.
5 You *didn't have to*/*mustn't* take part in yesterday's demonstration.
6 How much money do you think I *ought to*/*have to* donate?
7 If you want to sign the petition, you'll *need to*/*must* do it soon as I'm posting it off today.
8 The government has warned companies that they *don't have to*/*mustn't* break the law.

1 Listen to a radio programme about wildlife charities. Are the statements *true* or *false*?

1   NGO stands for National Government Organisation.   *false*
2   Elephant Family is a large NGO.
3   Over twenty NGOs are involved in the conservation of Asian elephants.
4   NGOs spend $4m a year on this conservation effort.
5   A report found that the most efficient NGOs were the largest.

2 Put the words in the correct order to make phrases used to make a case and influence your listener's opinion.

1   considered /you /that /have   *have you considered that...*
2   know /all /we /about
3   that /I /you /sure /am /agree /would
4   that /means /surely /that
5   have /we /to /that /remember
6   obvious /that /is /it

3 Now look at the audioscript on page 85 and underline the phrases above.

Writing You are involved in a wildlife campaign. Write an email (50–80 words) to a friend asking for help with the campaign. Include:

–   details of when you need help
–   information about what you are doing on that day
–   a request for your friend to invite more people to join you
–   your contact details.

Then compare your answer with the suggested answer on page 95.

Reading **1** Read the article on the opposite page quickly and choose the most appropriate title.

Major new ban on chemicals
Victory for environmentalists
Campaigners disappointed

2 Now complete the article with the sentences below.

Plans to regulate the chemicals industry in Europe approved by the European Commission on October 29th are a minor victory for industrial lobbyists over environmental campaigners. "I can live with it," was the less than enthusiastic comment by Margot Wallström, the Environment Commissioner, who had wanted something far more ambitious. ¹___*d*___ He claimed that the right balance had now been struck between growth and employment on the one hand and health and the environment on the other.

Behind the Commission's proposal is the fear that the world is full of unknown chemicals doing damage to health and happiness. It proposes that any business making or importing more than one tonne per year of a chemical must register safety information on a central database. Those chemicals seen as riskiest to health or the environment, or produced in the greatest quantity, will be subject to evaluation by the authorities. ²_____.

But the Commission has given in too easily to industry,

say the greens. ³_____. These three politicians jointly wrote to Romano Prodi, the Commission President, giving warning of the dangers of excessive regulation. So how far have the Commission's original proposals changed? A requirement to provide safety information for some 20,000 chemicals produced in quantities of less than ten tonnes per year. Also, a requirement to switch to alternative chemicals is now less binding. ⁴_____. And there will be fewer limits on what can be imported into the EU.

Yet still the chemicals industry continues to complain that European producers will be put at a competitive disadvantage. This is because restrictions are not as strict elsewhere, particularly on chemicals that have long been in widespread use.

The lobbying battle will now move into international arenas like the European Parliament and the Council of Ministers. ⁵_____. While it goes on, the Commission should think about what it is doing. Increasingly, it justifies its actions by saying that it is trying to protect consumers. ⁶_____. For Europe's three biggest economies, the price proposed was much too high.

a The process could easily take another few years.

b Very dangerous chemicals, such as carcinogens, will need authorisation before use.

c Firms will have the right to keep some information about products confidential.

d Her colleague, Erkki Liikanen, the Commissioner for Enterprise, was happier.

e But the fight over chemicals has shown that consumer protection comes at a price.

f Pro-industry lobbyists include Gerhard Schröder, Jacques Chirac and Tony Blair.

3 Look at the article again. Find the adjective of the following nouns.

industrial
industry   environment   enthusiasm   ambition   risk
excess   origin   alternative   competition

Unit 13 Communication

Vocabulary: **Communication**
Language: **Reported speech**
Career skills: **Summarising**
Writing: **Email summarising a message**

Vocabulary

1 Which of the verbs does not match each noun?.

1 AN EMAIL
   a send   **b** receive   **c** <u>present</u>   **d** open   **e** write

2 INFORMATION
   a access   **b** analyse   **c** process   **d** give   **e** correspond

3 A PROBLEM
   a spend   **b** deal with   **c** handle   **d** solve   **e** identify

4 A PHONE CALL
   a make   **b** receive   **c** return   **d** answer   **e** communicate

5 A MESSAGE
   a send   **b** respond   **c** take   **d** leave   **e** return

6 TIME
   a report   **b** waste   **c** prioritise   **d** manage   **e** spend

2 Match the pairs.

1 voice   **a** message
2 cell   **b** mail
3 text   **c** phone
4 mobile   **d** machine
5 fax   **e** phone
6 paper   **f** technology
7 information   **g** mail
8 snail   **h** work

3 Complete the table below.

	verb	noun
1	communicate	*communication*
2		announcement
3	interrupt	
4		correspondence
5		response

4 Use the clues to find the words in the puzzle.

1 deal with (information etc.)
2 free and continuous movement
3 system for saving and playing phone messages
4 exchange of information by telephone or cable
5 give a brief statement of the main points
6 disturbing to privacy
7 formal set of guidelines
8 protection from risk or danger
9 excess of information
10 pass information from one place to another
11 great quantity that all comes at the same time

1				P	R	O	C	E	S	S				
2							O							
3							M							
4							M							
5							U							
6							N							
7							I							
8							C							
9							A							
10							T							
11							E							

Listening 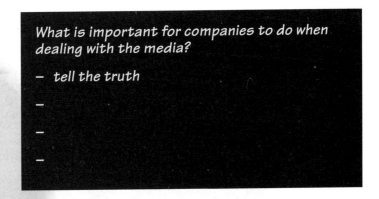 T17 **1** Look at the unfinished slide below. What additional points would you make in a short presentation on this topic?

What is important for companies to do when dealing with the media?

- tell the truth

-

-

-

2 Now listen to a manager speaking about this topic. What points does he mention? Were any points the same as yours?

1 **Complete the sentences using reported speech.**

1 'Have you seen Janis Browne, the Communications Manager?'
My colleague asked me if ...
I had seen Janis Browne, the Communications Manager.

2 'I can attend the training session.'
Marlon said ...

3 'The meeting won't take long.'
My manager confirmed that ...

4 'Should I book the the conference room for 2pm?'
My colleague asked ...

5 'I may have to leave work early because of a doctor's appointment.'
Callum explained that ...

6 'I'm meeting Andy for lunch.'
Pete said ...

7 'We have to be at the airport by 9.45.'
My boss told us ...

8 'If I were you, I'd take a break.'
My colleague advised ...

2 **Put the sentences in the correct order to make a voicemail message from Susan Hill.**

a I'm supposed to be meeting him at 11 o'clock. ☐

b The thing is, my train was delayed. ☐

c This is Susan Hill calling from Wantage Ltd at 10am. ☐ 1

d Anyway, please can Jamie call me on my mobile. ☐

e I'd like to leave a message for Jamie Parsons. ☐

f That's why I'm running a little late. ☐

g My number's 07889 021021. Er, thank you. Bye. ☐

You are a colleague of Jamie Parsons. He is working from home before a meeting and has asked you to check any voicemail messages on his office phone for him. Write an email (30–50 words) to Jamie summarising Susan's message. Then compare your answer with the suggested answer on page 96.

1 Suzanne Jameson, Communications Manager at LWP, is interviewed about electronic communications (email, internet and intranet). Listen and choose the correct options a–c.

1 According to Suzanne, companies use intranets to   *b*
  a reduce company costs.
  b motivate their employees.
  c keep teams in contact with each other.

2 Which statement does Suzanne make?
  a The majority of staff do not have the same first language.
  b Many employees work away from their workplace.
  c Key vacancies are filled by the wrong people.

3 Which of these advantages of an intranet is mentioned?
  a Companies can monitor staff contact with suppliers.
  b It is a way of providing free training courses.
  c Everyone can receive the same information.

4 How does Ford's management use the company intranet?
  a to inform staff about company business
  b to provide technical support
  c to recruit new staff

5 What problem arose at SAP?
  a The Chairman felt he was losing control.
  b Employees thought the intranet was a waste of time.
  c Some middle managers were unhappy about changed roles.

6 Which statement is made about communication at Siemens?
  a Arrangements are all made by secretaries.
  b All emails go via the Chief Information Officer.
  c Everyone has the right to communicate across the organisation.

2 Now complete the phrases to summarise Suzanne's views from the interview. Remember to summarise Suzanne's message – not necessarily her words.

1 Suzanne was talking about ...   *the effect of new technology on communication.*

2 Basically, what Suzanne said was that intranets ...

3 She reckons that ...

4 When asked about potential disadvantages of technology, she said the main thing is ...

Unit 14 Logistics

Vocabulary:	**Logistics**
Language:	**Passives**
Career skills:	**Dealing with questions**
Writing:	**Letter replying to a request for information**

Language check

1 Read the article about logistics. Use the headings to make notes comparing past and modern-day practices.

logistics in the past	logistics now
batches of products used to stay in warehouses until needed then sit in warehouses once dispatched	

The Economist

Business

A moving story

A wider view of logistics

Logistics is a word that [1]*is seen* / *sees* most often on the side of trucks. But it has a bigger meaning: how the flow of materials through an organisation, from raw materials to finished goods, [2]*is managed* / *manages*. Logistics might sound a simple enough business of moving things around, but it [3]*is growing* / *is being grown* more complex as customers demand better services, and as new technology and greater use of the internet [4]*are opened up* / *open up* new ways of passing around information.

The Japanese-led methods of lean production and just-in-time supplies tended [5]*to be kept* / *to keep* within factory walls. Following production, outgoing products [6]*were delivered* / *delivered* to distributors in batches, only to sit around in warehouses. Now, however, companies are more demanding, seeking to eliminate both incoming and outgoing inventory. This [7]*does* / *is done* in several ways. For example, in order to simplify what [8]*goes* / *is gone* into the

factory, companies [9]*buy* / *are bought* in sub-assemblies rather than individual parts. Companies are also trying to build to order (BTO) only, rather than guessing what will be in demand and supplying orders from existing stocks. But to cut inventories and introduce BTO, a comprehensive, flexible freight operation [10]*requires* / *is required*. This is such a challenging task that companies are reluctant to do it all themselves, which is why more and more of them are [11]*outsourcing* / *being outsourced* delivery and logistics to third parties.

This movement [12]*is forcing* / *is being forced* the freight transport industry to change. Manufacturers want custom-designed delivery systems, using all types of transport: land, sea and air. The distinction between postal, express and logistics services [13]*has almost vanished* / *has almost been vanished*. And the fastest growing area of business is outsourced third-party logistics.

2 Now underline the correct active or passive forms in italics.

1 Match the words with the definitions.

1	monitor	a	have no more supplies
2	freight	b	check over a period of time
3	flow	c	transporting goods by road in lorries
4	pallet	d	goods transported by road, air or sea
5	run out	e	continuous smooth movement
6	haulage	f	wooden platform for carrying goods

2 Which is the odd one out in each set?

	a	b	c
1	customer	<u>court</u>	client
2	stock	inventory	shelf
3	pilot	scan	test
4	supermarket	factory	warehouse
5	image	tag	microchip
6	chain	cargo	freight
7	goods	figures	products
8	trace	track	try
9	shipping	access	delivery
10	lorry	rail	truck

3 Match the pairs.

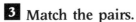

1	smart	a	materials
2	consumer	b	tag
3	bar	c	strategy
4	conveyor	d	chain
5	loading	e	bay
6	raw	f	code
7	supply	g	goods
8	marketing	h	belt

4 How many verbs can you find in the unit that can go before *product*? Add them to the word map.

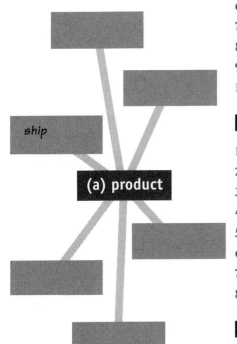

ship

(a) product

1 Read the article about the use of new technology in logistics. Six companies are mentioned. What is the name of each? What type of business is it involved in?

	company	type of business
1	FedEx	logistics company
2		
3		
4		
5		
6		

The Economist

Business

New technology

Automation is part of it, but better understanding is the key

New technology is influencing the way logistics companies are doing business – and cutting their costs. For example, it costs FedEx $2.40 to track a package for a [1] _customer_ who calls by phone, but only four cents for one who visits its website, says Rob Carter, the firm's technology boss. FedEx now gets about 3m [2]_____ tracking requests a day, compared with only a few tens of thousands by phone.

But the most dramatic gains happen when companies use technology to understand better what they do in order to change how they do it, says Navi Radjou, an analyst at Forrester, a technology research firm. The main issue is 'grandma syndrome' – a reluctance to get rid of tried and [3]_____ processes. The brave company fighting this syndrome is probably Dell, the computer maker. It constantly improves the way that it links customers and [4]_____ through its website, and it regularly revisits its processes. Dell now sends electronic orders to suppliers every few hours and can build a computer in less than 24. One of its managers in Austin, Texas, was recently heard estimating gains of 30% this year, and again next year.

A member of a team from the car makers Ford recently visiting Dell doubted that his employer could ever do anything so drastic. But old-established companies can make similar [5]_____. Procter & Gamble, the consumer [6]_____ giant, used to think that the most efficient way to get detergent from its [7]_____ to shops was to load trucks as fully as possible. Then, a few years ago, it invested in software, now owned by a company called Nutech Solutions, to simulate what happened to its orders as they moved through the supply [8]_____. The unexpected conclusion was that it makes more sense to send trucks less full, and to load some toothpaste and other stuff alongside the detergent. As a result, P&G's inventory is down by some 30%, and its warehouse workers spend less time idle.

2 Now complete the article with the following words.

goods   customer   suppliers   online   tested   chain   gains   warehouses

3 Read the article again. Are the statements *true* or *false*?

1   It is expensive for FedEx to track orders for internet users.   *false*
2   FedEx has twice as many telephone tracking requests as online ones.
3   Dell regularly evaluates and updates the way it does things.
4   Dell has taken on 30% more staff to deal with increased business.
5   Proctor and Gamble has changed the way it dispatches its goods.
6   Proctor and Gamble now needs fewer warehouse workers.

Listening T19 **1** Which of these areas do you think you would find most difficult to talk about at a job interview?

a   your reasons for leaving your current employment
b   your attitude and approach to your work
c   your past achievements
d   your ability to deal with feedback
e   your ability to work with other people
f   your opinion about industry or professional trends
g   your salary expectations
h   your expectations for the future

2 Now listen to eight questions from an interview. Match each question with an area above. Then decide how you would answer each question.

1	*b*	5	☐
2	☐	6	☐
3	☐	7	☐
4	☐	8	☐

Listening T20 Listen to a voicemail message and complete the notes.

Name of caller: Melanie **(1)** ...   Reilly
Company: Kell Ltd, 76 High St, Minton, MI10 8RT
Message:
Said thanks for the **(2)** ...
Is interested in stocking model number **(3)** ...
Wants to know price for 50 plus payment and **(4)** ... terms

Writing   Now write a letter (50–70 words) replying to Melanie's message. Ensure you answer each of her points. Then compare your answer with the suggested answer on page 96.

Unit 15 Innovation

Pushing the limits

Vocabulary:	**Innovation**
Language:	**Past modals**
Career skills:	**Reviewing achievement**
Writing:	**Letter nominating someone for an award**

Vocabulary

1 **Which is the odd one out in each set?**

1	**a** profit	**b** <u>failure</u>	**c** reward	**d** margin
2	**a** accomplishment	**b** disaster	**c** breakthrough	**d** achievement
3	**a** transform	**b** adapt	**c** research	**d** modify
4	**a** flop	**b** dud	**c** fiasco	**d** design
5	**a** devise	**b** invent	**c** predict	**d** come up with
6	**a** feature	**b** boundary	**c** frontier	**d** threshold

2 **Match the pairs.**

1	business	**a**	alley
2	critical	**b**	practice
3	blind	**c**	seller
4	bottom	**d**	development
5	best	**e**	market
6	product	**f**	place
7	market	**g**	line
8	target	**h**	factor

3 **Match the verbs with the nouns.**

1	develop	**a**	time
2	pay	**b**	a system
3	waste	**c**	risks
4	build	**d**	research
5	find	**e**	a product
6	take	**f**	a prototype
7	set	**g**	interest
8	carry out	**h**	a problem
9	launch	**i**	a solution
10	solve	**j**	a trend

1 Read the article about innovation. Are the statements *true* or *false*?

1 Most successful innovations are by individuals. *false*
2 Successful innovators take advantage of opportunities that arise from change.
3 Of the forms of change discussed by Drucker, more than half happen within a company.
4 Returns from successful knowledge-based innovations are usually about 16%.
5 Companies can expect only 100 successful innovations from 3,000 original ideas.

The Economist

Business

Innovation by numbers

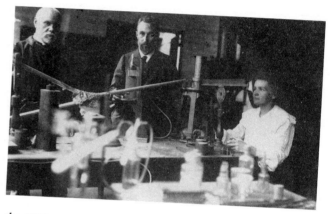

Innovation or improvement?

Where would the world be today without the (¹invent) _invention_ of controllable, powered flight by the Wright brothers, or the (²discover) _____ of penicillin by Sir Alexander Fleming? But these are exceptions. The majority of successful (³innovate) _____ haven't come from individuals. They've come from team efforts organised by companies exploiting change. That change can take many forms.

Peter Drucker identifies seven such forms of change, the four most important of which are all within the enterprise itself. The first is unexpected (⁴succeed) _____ or failure. The second is the gap between what actually happens and what is supposed to happen. The third is the inadequacy in an existing process that is taken for granted. The fourth is changes in industrial and market structure that take everyone by surprise. As for the three sources of innovation that occur outside the enterprise, they are: changes in demographics, changes in perception, and finally changes caused by new (⁵know) _____.

So why do innovators innovate? For a variety of reasons: the glamour of an R&D breakthrough or the gambler's dream of winning millions, for example. Certainly, for the few who get it right, innovations based on the (⁶apply) _____ of new knowledge can have huge rewards. One American study found that the annual return from 17 successful technological innovations made during

the 1970s averaged 56%. That compares with a 16% average return on (⁷invest) _____ for all of American business in the years since then.

Genentech, a biotech firm in Silicon Valley, has spent 15 years and almost $1 billion searching for a particular cancer drug. But when positive results from trials of Genentech's new colon cancer drug, Avastin, were announced in May, investors quickly added $15 billion to the company's market value. Those are the kind of winnings Genentech could get from the new drug before the (⁸expire) _____ of its patent.

But to achieve such returns from technological innovations, companies such as Genentech, Intel and Microsoft have to employ huge numbers of (⁹research) _____. An enterprise has to start with around 3,000 bright ideas if it is to come up with 100 worthwhile projects, which will then be reduced to four (¹⁰develop) _____ programmes. And four such programmes are the minimum needed to stand any chance of getting one winner.

2 Now complete the article using the correct form of the words in brackets.

3 Look at the article again. Find the opposites of the following words.

1 minority *majority*
2 success
3 adequacy
4 inside
5 losing
6 negative
7 tiny
8 increased

1 Look at the sentences with past modal verbs. Find and correct the mistakes.

have

1 I think I may ~~had~~ made a mistake in the calculations.
2 We waited too long. We should have patent our new process immediately.
3 With more time and money, we could won the competition.
4 You shouldn't spent have so much time on one particular idea.
5 If they'd had more support, it might had been easier for them.
6 What could I have did to improve my design?

2 Complete the sentences appropriately with the correct past form of the modal verb.

1 I went without any new brochures. I should ...   *have taken some.*
2 Everyone here blames James for crashing the computer system. I'm not so sure. He may ...
3 I ate so much at the business lunch that I feel quite ill. I shouldn't ...
4 My boss didn't ask me to write the report, but I could ...
5 I'm afraid John's not here. I don't know where he is. He might ...
6 We're really grateful for the grant we received as it allowed us to focus on new product development. Without the grant, we mightn't ...
7 Jason didn't attend the launch although he was free . He could ...
8 We tried to be too revolutionary. That's why the new product failed. We probably should ...

3 Put the words in the correct order to make sentences reviewing achievement. Then decide which sentences offer praise (P) and which offer criticism (C).

1 spoken /you /to /don't /I /manager /think /should /the /have
   I don't think you should have spoken to the manager. (C)
2 complete /to /time /able /come /how /you /weren't /on /project /the?
3 led /how /by /really /I'm /impressed /you /meeting /the
4 with /job /a /new /done /range /you've /great /the
5 by /little /current /a /disappointed /your /I'm /performance
6 job /better /have /could /no-one /done /a

Listening ⊙ T21

1 Listen to part of a radio programme about innovation. The speaker talks about the features of successful and less successful innovations. Make notes on them below.

successful innovations	less successful innovations
moderately new to the market	*based on cutting edge technology*

2 What event does the speaker refer to?

3 Now complete the sentences with *by, to, about, in, of* or *on*. Then check your answers in the audioscript on page 87.

1 A very good explanation ____*of*____ this can be found in an interesting study.

2 Successful innovations were based _____ tried and tested technology.

3 The products that failed had no clearly defined solution _____ mind.

4 What we're talking _____ is a new way of looking at things to meet a real need.

5 That brings me on _____ news of an event organised by *The Economist*.

6 That'll be followed _____ the announcement of the winners.

Writing

Read the extract and then write a letter (80–120 words) to *The Economist* nominating an innovator for an award. Include the following information:

– the name of the innovator
– the award category you are entering the person for
– brief background information about the innovator
– the benefits of one of their recent innovations
– a reference to further details about the innovator
– your contact details.

Then compare your answer with the suggested answer on page 96.

The Economist's annual Innovation Awards recognise talented innovators in the categories of biotech, computing, energy/environment, and telecoms. Readers who wish to nominate innovators should do so by July 5th. The winners will be announced at The Economist's Innovation Summit and Awards in San Francisco on September 23rd.

In order to nominate an innovator for this award, please write to The Economist at the following address:

BEC Vantage practice test

Introduction to BEC (Business English Certificate) Vantage

This workbook contains a complete BEC Vantage practice test (on pages 66–79). The BEC Vantage examination is a Cambridge ESOL (UCLES) business English examination at approximately intermediate level. BEC Vantage consists of four components: reading, writing, listening and speaking.

Reading test

Different parts of the Reading paper test different reading skills. Part 1 tests reading for gist and scanning. Part 2 tests your ability to understand text structure; in order to do this you are required to fill a gapped text with sentences. Part 3 tests your ability to read for gist and understand specific information. Part 4 tests your vocabulary. Part 5 is a proofreading task, where you are required to identify extra words in a short text.

When preparing for the examination it is useful to:

– practise reading as many types of documents as you can

– make sure you understand the use of reference words (like *this*, *such* and *it*)

– record useful vocabulary and fixed phrases linked to different business topics

– check your own work and keep a record of the typical mistakes you make

– exchange your written work with a fellow student and check his/her work for errors.

Writing test

The Writing paper tests short neutral/informal writing in Part 1 (e.g. an email to a colleague) and longer neutral/formal writing in Part 2 (e.g. a letter to a client). It is important in the Writing paper that you:

– answer the question that is set

– use a variety of grammatical structures and vocabulary accurately and appropriately

– make sure that your writing is clear and well structured

– write concisely and pay attention to the suggested number of words.

Listening test

The Listening paper tests a variety of listening skills, for example listening for gist (identifying topic, context etc.) in Part 2, and listening for both main ideas and specific information in Part 3. When preparing for the examination you should:

– get as much listening practice as possible

– practise taking notes when you are making telephone calls (this will help you with Part 1)

– consider the following as you listen to English: who the speakers might be, what their role is, what the purpose of the conversation is etc.

Speaking test

The Speaking paper tests different skills. In Part 1 you are tested on your ability to talk about yourself (work, interests etc.). Try to answer the questions as fully as possible.

In Part 2 you choose one of three business topics and give a 'mini-presentation' (for approximately one minute) on the topic. Before you start your presentation, you are given a minute to prepare what you want to say; it is a good idea to make brief notes during this time. At the end of the presentation, the other candidate can ask you a question; give as full an answer as you can. During your presentation, it is important that you:

– outline your main points clearly and refer to them in a logical order

– give reasons for your points.

In Part 3 of the Speaking paper you are asked to discuss a given topic with another candidate. It is important that you:

– give your opinion on the topic and give reasons for your opinions

– ask the other candidate for his/her opinions.

The tables on page 65 describe the components of the BEC Vantage examination. The final columns refer you to units with workbook exercises which are similar in format to BEC Vantage tasks. You may find it useful to focus on them if you are preparing for the examination.

Reading test (60 minutes)

Part	Type of reading	Task	Number of questions	Workbook units
1	Gist and scanning	Matching sentences with texts	7	Unit 11
2	Understanding text structure	Matching sentences with gaps in text	5	Units 1 and 12
3	Gist and specific understanding	Multiple choice comprehension questions	6	Unit 10
4	Vocabulary and structure	Multiple choice gap filling	15	Units 4, 6 and 7
5	Finding errors	Proofreading (finding extra words)	12	Units 5 and 8

Writing test (45 minutes)

Part	Task	Word length	Workbook units
1	Writing a short email, fax, message, memo or note	40–50 words	Units 1, 3, 5, 6, 10, 11, 12, 13 and 14
2	Writing a longer letter, fax, report or proposal	120–140 words	Units 9 and 15

Listening test (40 minutes including 10 minutes to transfer answers to a separate sheet)

Part	Type of listening	Task	Number of questions	Workbook units
1	Three telephone conversations or messages	Gap filling	12	Unit 14
2	Identifying topic, purpose etc. of short monologues	Multiple matching	10	Unit 2
3	Answering questions based on a longer conversation	Multiple choice comprehension questions	8	Unit 13

Speaking test (14 minutes)

Part	Task	Time	Workbook units
1	Giving information about yourself (work, hobbies etc.)	About 3 minutes	Unit 1
2	Giving a 'mini-presentation' about a business topic	About 6 minutes	Unit 13
3	Discussion with another candidate on a given topic	About 5 minutes	Unit 7

READING

PART ONE

Questions 1 – 7

- Look at the statements below and the extracts from an article about financial irregularities.

- Which section (**A, B, C** or **D**) does each statement refer to?

- For each statement **1 – 7**, mark one letter (**A, B, C** or **D**).

- You will need to use some of these letters more than once.

Example

One auditing firm has announced that it has increased its turnover by 30%.   *C*

---

1   To remain in business, auditing firms need to offer a larger range of services.

2   Experience shows that problems can arise when the same firm has audited a client's accounts for some time.

3   A senior executive is currently in court for accounting irregularities.

4   Some people argue it could be negative for companies to vary the firm employed to carry out audits.

5   One auditor has been accused of destroying vital financial documents.

6   Regulations now limit the range of work that audit firms can provide for a particular company.

7   There is a concern among regulators that standard company audits have suffered because auditors prefer to offer high-cost consultancy services.

A

There is still no end to the corporate scandals affecting the USA, many of which have raised questions about the role of large auditing firms. Dennis Kozlowski, the former boss of Tyco, now on trial for defrauding his old company, is trying to push responsibility on to Tyco's auditor, PricewaterhouseCoopers. Last month, a former partner of Ernst & Young was arrested for shredding documents related to the audit of NextCard, an online credit-card issuer that went bankrupt. Other members of the Big Four, the firms that dominate auditing worldwide, have also worked with companies accused of accounting fraud.

B

Auditing reform started when the Sarbanes-Oxley Act was passed with the aim of restoring investors' trust following major accounting frauds such as the scandal at Enron. Regulators worried that the attraction of fat consulting fees had affected the quality of plain, low-margin audits, and concluded that long-term relationships between companies and accountants had a negative effect on book-keeping standards. Almost all the biggest accounting irregularities, including those at Enron and Tyco, occurred under auditors who had been on the job for at least a decade.

C

New rules passed by the SEC in January ban auditors from providing certain consulting services for audit clients and oblige them to change the senior partner in charge of each audit every five years. Nevertheless, auditors can still provide profitable extras, such as tax planning, to clients. Ernst & Young reported that its annual revenues had jumped by almost a third, mainly due to non-audit services. Critics argue that the reforms are not enough. They say that only changing auditing firms, not just partners, will keep auditors and their clients from getting too comfortable.

D

Providing tax and other consulting services, says the industry, improves audits by helping auditors gain detailed knowledge of the companies they monitor. And, because auditing is a low-margin business burdened with enormous risk of legal action, and therefore insurance costs, auditors must diversify in order to survive. Accountants also point out that obliging companies to change auditing firms regularly would lead to higher costs and poorer quality as new auditors struggle with unfamiliar businesses.

PART TWO

Questions 8 – 12

- Read the article below about innovation.

- Choose the best sentence below to fill each of the gaps.

- For each gap **8 – 12**, mark one letter **(A – G)**.

- Do not use any letter more than once.

- There is an example at the beginning, **(0)**.

Innovation is rarely rocket science

Next month Gillette will launch the successor to its very successful Mach3 razor. Although the company would like it to be as revolutionary as the Mach3 was in its day, the latest version is unlikely be more than evolutionary. That might not, however, prevent it from making a large contribution to Gillette's profits. These days, great fortunes can be made from seemingly modest innovations.

Big firms still hope for great breakthrough inventions – products that will contribute to their profits for at least a decade. They are, however, coming up with fewer and fewer such inventions. **(0)** ...*B*.... Indeed, in the past, small firms have been responsible for the majority of breakthrough products. The USA's Small Business Administration claims that the personal computer and the Polaroid camera came from small entrepreneurial organisations – and these are only some of the products from a list of items beginning with the letter 'p'.

(8) .... That is to say they are generally more able to improve the ways in which products invented elsewhere are manufactured, marketed and continually improved. Most of the companies that have created huge amounts of wealth have done so by inventing great processes, not great products. **(9)** ....

So what implications does this have for big firms? Does this mean they should sack all their scientists and leave inventing to others? **(10)** .... For some time the computer industry has, in effect, relied for much of its research and development on small firms supported by external capital. And the telecoms industry is outsourcing more and more research to smaller firms in India and elsewhere.

Without their own research labs, however, big firms fear that they may be taken by surprise and have their businesses ruined by a revolutionary innovation invented by an entrepreneur. But, as history has shown time and time again, employing in-house scientists and researchers provides no guarantee that their work will protect the company from technological change. **(11)** .... It is far better if managers in big corporations keep an eye on the outside world and their minds open to any new ideas they see there. **(12)** .... They can find innovative ways to bring them to market and thereby guarantee future sources of income for their employers.

A   Dell, Toyota and Wal-Mart, for example, have succeeded by coming up with efficient ways of getting ordinary products into the hands of consumers more cheaply than their rivals.

B   That explains the high number of researchers leaving big firms.

C   In practice, more and more are doing just that.

D   Xerox, AT&T and IBM, for instance, spent millions on such research, but were all overtaken by new technologies.

E   Big firms are better at less dramatic forms of innovation.

F   They can then buy them and do what they do best.

G   This is despite the fact that large companies within many industries, particularly pharmaceuticals, continue to spend large sums trying.

PART THREE

Questions 13 – 18

- Read the article below about business education courses.
- For each question **13 – 18**, mark one letter **(A, B, C** or **D)** for the answer you choose.

Creating leaders

1   In America, business schools have long aimed to provide general business education for a career as a leader or manager in the form of the Masters in Business Administration (MBA). By the late 1990s, such schools were turning out 100,000 MBA graduates a year, compared with 13,000 in Britain and only 1,400 in Germany. Mr Khurana, who is currently writing a book on the evolution of management as a profession, points out that a growing proportion of business people now have an MBA – as indeed does President George Bush.

2   However, the MBA has few of the characteristics of traditional professional training. For example, it involves no promise to follow professional standards, as seen with qualifications in law, medicine, auditing and accountancy. There is also no commitment to taking shorter follow-up courses as part of the professional's continuing education. Worse, argues Mr Khurana, some of the theories taught in business schools conflict with a sense of professionalism. For example, if managers are 'agents', shareholders are 'principals' and organisations simply process contracts, the implication is that a manager has an obligation to fulfil a contract, as does a consultant or an investment banker, but owes no loyalty to a larger body, which is one of the characteristics of a professional.

3   A further criticism of MBA courses is that they may be more useful at training people to advise large complex corporations than to run them. Certainly, many companies seem critical of the courses that business schools teach. When INSEAD, a top-ranking business school near Paris, asked the companies whose managers it educates what they wanted, it found the answer was increased hands-on experience, less analysis and fewer case studies.

4   So schools are redesigning their courses. The Sloan School at MIT is offering MBA students a three-day workshop on 'visioning' and role-playing, and a selection of compulsory leadership courses, including one on leading in an entrepreneurial firm. There is a course on self-assessment, and the option to work for an organisation, create change, and be coached on how they are doing.

5   Such changes may help business schools to retain clients, especially for executive education, which has been one of their most profitable sidelines. But companies often want to teach their up-and-coming leaders themselves. Many now have programmes loosely modelled on GE's in-house academy, Crotonville, founded by Ralph Cordiner, who ran the company in the 1950s. Chief executives such as Jorma Ollila at Nokia and J T Battenberg of Delphi, a large car parts company, personally teach on such courses.

6   Noel Tichy, a guru at the University of Michigan, cleverly runs a course to teach business leaders to run their own courses. He points out that most business school staff are researchers with little real-world experience. "Leadership is a clinical art, and people need experience," he argues. "You don't train a physician by getting a researcher to perform open-heart surgery."

7   Whether people can learn to be leaders from traditional business school courses is questionable. Most people probably learn largely on the job, by watching and by making mistakes, as they have always done.

13 According to the text, in the 1990s

    A George Bush graduated with an MBA.

    B more business schools were founded than at any other time.

    C Khurana wrote a book about the development of management studies.

    D there were more MBA graduates in America than in Britain and Germany together.

14 How do MBA courses compare with other professional training?

    A MBA studies are broader, with students selecting modules from other professional courses.

    B Entry standards for MBA programmes are lower than with other professional education.

    C Graduates from MBA courses do not belong to a professional group.

    D MBAs are shorter than other professional training courses.

15 Feedback on INSEAD courses revealed that

    A experienced managers appreciate being given the opportunity to teach at INSEAD.

    B companies would like to see more practical work on INSEAD courses.

    C graduates from INSEAD often become corporate consultants.

    D INSEAD teachers are considered the best in their field.

16 What change has the Sloan School at MIT introduced?

    A Students now have to take courses on being a leader.

    B It is bringing in a prolonged assessment of students' abilities.

    C There are opportunities for students to gain experience as a business coach.

    D Practical experience of managing change is compulsory for Sloan School students.

17 Which statement is true of paragraph 5?

    A Clients want training at their own companies to follow the MBA model.

    B Chief executives offer to teach on the new business school courses.

    C Many companies still prefer to run in-house courses.

    D MBA courses are increasingly profitable.

18 Which statement is true of Noel Tichy?

    A He learns a lot on courses by business leaders.

    B He questions the expertise of some business school staff.

    C He teaches business skills to medical students.

    D He praises the quality of research in business schools.

PART FOUR

Questions 19 – 33

- Read the article below about a leading name in British business.

- Choose the best word to fill each gap from **A, B, C** or **D** below.

- For each question **19 – 33**, mark one letter (**A, B, C** or **D**).

- There is an example at the beginning, (**0**).

A reasonable job?

Sir Peter Davis became (**0**) .B. executive of the British supermarket firm J. Sainsbury in March 2000. He had left 14 years earlier, when Sainsbury was one of Britain's greatest businesses, a chain of national supermarkets that (**19**) … quality with value – as reflected in its 'good food costs less' (**20**) …. By March 2000, when Sir Peter rejoined the firm, Sainsbury was in crisis: profits and (**21**) … were falling. Under the two previous bosses, Sainsbury had lost market leadership to its (**22**) … Tesco. Sir Peter had run Reed International and Prudential Insurance successfully, helping Prudential to (**23**) … from a crisis of its own. Surely he would now save Sainsbury.

But a few years later, (**24**) … of admiration, Sir Peter now attracts criticism. Investors are unhappy about the recent (**25**) … to him of extra shares worth £3.9m, and about the decision of the (**26**) … to make him chairman next March. The share (**27**) … has fallen behind its sector by 17% since Sir Peter arrived. Sir Peter has, in fact, done a reasonable job. He has (**28**) … costs and raised profits, and savings are on (**29**) … to reach £960m by 2005. Yet disappointment came on June 24th, when Britain's competition regulator suggested that Sainsbury would not be allowed to (**30**) … up market share by buying Safeway, another supermarket chain. All these problems have arisen (**31**) … Sir Peter has invested up to £2 billion to modernise stores and IT infrastructure at Sainsbury. Arguably, there has been too little investment in genuine (**32**) … which would allow Sainsbury to stand out from other supermarkets. Another error may have been to fail to increase non-food sales, which account for just 13% of (**33**) … at Sainsbury, compared with 18% at Tesco and a fifth at Asda, the supermarket chains that might be regarded as a model for Sainsbury.

0	**A** main	**B** chief	**C** head	**D** lead
19	**A** joined	**B** combined	**C** mixed	**D** linked
20	**A** logo	**B** image	**C** slogan	**D** brand
21	**A** margins	**B** edges	**C** thresholds	**D** frontiers
22	**A** opposition	**B** rival	**C** competition	**D** opponent
23	**A** improve	**B** repair	**C** progress	**D** recover
24	**A** other	**B** except	**C** instead	**D** rather
25	**A** award	**B** prize	**C** gift	**D** reward
26	**A** group	**B** committee	**C** agency	**D** board
27	**A** cost	**B** rate	**C** figure	**D** price
28	**A** reduced	**B** slumped	**C** declined	**D** fallen
29	**A** objective	**B** goal	**C** target	**D** aim
30	**A** build	**B** extend	**C** grow	**D** enlarge
31	**A** although	**B** but	**C** however	**D** despite
32	**A** modification	**B** revival	**C** creation	**D** transformation
33	**A** acquisitions	**B** gain	**C** turnover	**D** contracts

PART FIVE

Questions 34 – 45

- Read the article below about a survey of British managers.
- In most of the lines **34 – 45** there is one extra word. It is either grammatically incorrect or does not fit in with the sense of the text. Some lines, however, are correct.
- If a line is correct, write **CORRECT**.
- If there is an extra word in the line, write **the extra word** in CAPITAL LETTERS.
- The exercise begins with two examples (**0**) and (**00**).

Management survey

0	*THE*	According to a new survey by the magazine 'Management Today' nearly the half of
00	*CORRECT*	British managers would sacrifice £1,000 of their salary, their company car, private
34		medical insurance or a week's holiday for a more better workspace. The survey also
35		shows that 45% would consider moving to work for a competitor for to get a better
36		working environment. More than a quarter would therefore be ashamed to take a client
37		into their workplace. The survey found that people's expectations of such good
38		working conditions are not met by the companies they work for. This is despite of the
39		fact that managers are increasingly aware of the importance of workspace in reducing
40		stress, improving morale and driving up productivity. The survey also reveals so that
41		more than half of managers would prefer it a 'thinking space' to social facilities such
42		as a restaurant or shopping area. Public sector managers are more likely to have
43		facilities like a gym or that shower than their private sector counterparts. It is also
44		more probable than that they will benefit from flexible working practices. There is
45		greater willingness in the public sector to change jobs or trade annual leave for a better
		workspace than among private sector managers.

WRITING TEST

PART ONE

You are a sales manager at an IT firm. Jacob Mills, a client you have worked with for many years, has asked you to a meeting on 4th August. Write **an email** to the client:

- saying that you cannot make it on the date suggested

- giving your reasons

- suggesting an alternative date and time.

Write 40 – 50 words.

From:

To: Jacob Mills

subject: Meeting

PART TWO

- You work for a financial organisation. Your boss has sent you the email below and shown you the advertisement about offshoring.

- Look at the email and the advertisement, on which you have already made handwritten notes.

- Then, using **all** your handwritten notes, write an **email** to OFT.

- **Write 120 – 140 words.**

just admin services

Are you looking to offshore some or all of your business to India or China?

yes! – also info about China? advantages of India or China?

If so, look no further. Contact OFT International for expert advice at a reasonable price.

Call Daniel Davis on 07818 111331 or email Daniel_d@oft.com.

about recruiting staff, local costs, locations

ask for price list for their services

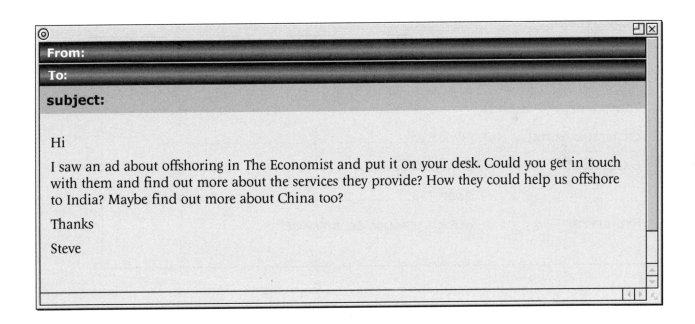

From:

To:

subject:

Hi

I saw an ad about offshoring in The Economist and put it on your desk. Could you get in touch with them and find out more about the services they provide? How they could help us offshore to India? Maybe find out more about China too?

Thanks

Steve

LISTENING

PART ONE (CD Track 22)

Questions 1 – 12

- You will hear three telephone conversations or messages.
- Write **one or two words or a number** in the numbered spaces on the notes or forms below.
- You will hear each recording twice.

Conversation One

(Questions 1 – 4)

- Look at the notes below.
- You will hear a woman calling an employment agency.

Notes

Company: PRO Ltd

Position vacant: (1) --

Department: (2) --

Details about position:

Temporary (4 mths)

Starting date: (3) --

Essential: degree/diploma

                good (4) -------------------------------- skills

Preferred: management experience

Conversation Two (CD Track 23)

(Questions 5 – 8)

- Look at the notes below.
- You will hear a woman calling a colleague.

Urgent!

Norcom has sacked its (5) -----------------------------------

(Oscar Case) because of illegal (6)---------------------------------- activities.

Arrange an urgent meeting to discuss action regarding any

(7) -------------------------------------.

Identify someone to be responsible for communication with the

(8) -------------------------------------.

Conversation Three (CD Track 24)

(Questions 9 – 12)

- Look at the notes below.
- You will hear a recorded message for a consultant.

Date and time of call: 3pm Thursday 10 June
Name of caller: Chris (9) ------------------------
Message for: Simon Marks

Notes

He says thank you for the feedback on the (10) --------------------.
Tuesday's meeting will look at the latest (11) ----------------------.
It will focus on how to attract more (12) ------------------------.
Please call Extension 324 to confirm attendance.

LISTENING

PART TWO (CD Track 25)

Questions 13 – 22

Section One

(Questions 13 – 17)

- You will hear five short recordings. Five people are talking about what they look for when they are buying goods from a company.

- For each recording, decide what each speaker is talking about.

- Write one letter (**A – H**) next to the number of the recording.

- Do not use any letter more than once.

- You will hear the five recordings twice.

13 ------------------------------

14 ------------------------------

15 ------------------------------

16 ------------------------------

17 ------------------------------

A good customer service

B telephone helpline

C efficient distribution

D extended guarantee

E simple ordering procedures

F value for money

G good reputation

H fashionable brand

Section Two (CD Track 26)

(Questions 18 – 22)

- You will hear another five short recordings. Each person is giving a presentation.

- For each recording, decide on the purpose of the presentation extract.

- Write one letter (**A – H**) next to the number of the recording.

- Do not use any letter more than once.

- You will hear the five recordings twice.

18 ------------------------------

19 ------------------------------

20 ------------------------------

21 ------------------------------

22 ------------------------------

A to announce record profits

B to advertise a new product

C to announce job losses

D to publicise job vacancies

E to confirm a pay rise

F to introduce a new policy

G to announce a merger

H to explain poor performance

PART THREE (CD Track 27)

Questions 23 – 30

- You will hear a radio interview about worker co-operatives.
- For each question **23-30**, mark one letter **A**, **B** or **C** for the correct answer.
- You will hear the recording twice.

23 What was the reaction to the employee buyout at Highlander?

    A Banks wanted to invest in the company.

    B The majority of clients were happy at the news.

    C A retail company expressed interest in a joint venture.

24 What are Highlander's plans following the buyout?

    A to increase its number of restaurants

    B to develop tourism in the local area

    C to take over some other firms

25 What does the speaker say about Muscovy?

    A It is planning to modernise its supermarket stores.

    B It sets retail trends that other companies follow.

    C It has benefited from recent developments in the market.

26 What is said about employee participation at Muscovy?

    A Employees do not take part in strategic decision-making.

    B Only certain types of employee are allowed to take part in voting.

    C Workers are involved in a wide range of decisions affecting the firm.

27 Which surprising fact is mentioned?

    A Banks can be confident about loaning money to worker-owned businesses.

    B Financial organisations have a negative attitude towards partnerships.

    C Employee-owned firms are unlikely to repay money they have borrowed.

28 What did Tony's study reveal about worker co-operatives?

    A There are more in Italy than elsewhere in Europe.

    B Co-operatives tend to employ more workers than other firms.

    C Towns with more co-operatives than usual are safer places to live.

29 What does Tony say when talking about the business he owned?

    A The paper-making industry is declining.

    B Worker participation promotes productivity.

    C His company recruited an extra 1,000 employees.

30 What did Tony's staff particularly like about worker co-operatives?

    A getting paid more

    B working flexible hours

    C feeling involved

SPEAKING TEST

PART ONE

Sample questions

What's your name?

Could you spell your name?

Where do you live?

What do you like about the place where you live? Why?

Do you like your job/studies?

What do you like best about your job/studies?

What's the most difficult thing for you about your job/studies?

How do you get to work/college?

What do you do in your free time?

PART TWO

A: WHAT IS IMPORTANT WHEN...?

Looking for a new job

- Salary
- Location
-
-

B: WHAT IS IMPORTANT WHEN...?

Leading a team

- Having clear goals
- Motivating people
-
-

C: WHAT IS IMPORTANT WHEN...?

Buying a product

- Price
- Quality
-
-

PART THREE

Launching an e-commerce product

Your company is going to launch a new e-commerce product.

You have been asked to help with the promotional campaign.

Discuss the situation together, and decide:

- what the campaign should include
- how to encourage customers to make repeat online purchases.

Audioscripts

Unit 1   **Companies** page 4

Listening 1 (Track 2)

S: Welcome to *Business World.* Tonight we have with us have special guest Chris Scott, author of *Leading Strategies.* Welcome to the studio, Chris.

C: Thank you, Sue.

S: We continue our series on the challenges facing today's business schools and how well they prepare their students for the real needs of the commercial world. Today we're focusing on Kellogg School of Management at Northwestern University. Chris, is it true that the Kellogg is considered America's top business school?

C: That's right, according to Business Week. And it's also rated the world's best by the Economist Intelligence Unit. It's got an excellent reputation not just amongst large international corporations who pay for all their senior staff to attend the school – but also among small and medium-sized enterprises, who sponsor maybe one or two key members of staff – and also with start-up companies, where the boss and founder of the company might fund his or her own studies.

S: What areas do the students traditionally work in?

C: Well, you get people from all areas of the company: customer services, finance, human resources, production, administration. It really varies.

Listening 2 (Track 3)

S: I hear that today's business school market is very tough. So, what kind of challenges are institutions like Kellogg facing?

C: Well, Sue, MBA students can no longer turn up for interviews certain that they'll receive a top job offer. Maybe this is partly because of a general reaction against a management elite after all the corporate scandals in recent years. But the stronger reason is probably because there's thought to be a big gap between what graduates of business schools can offer and what companies actually need.

S: You mean in terms of graduates' ability to actually apply the knowledge and skills they've acquired?

C: Yes. That's one reason why Kellogg has made some changes to its courses recently. One aim is to allow students to specialise sooner, hopefully making them more useful to employers. And another key change, reflecting the reality of business life, is that a class on 'leadership in times of crisis', which used to be optional, is now mandatory. Oh, and there are also a few new courses, for example on 'ethics' and 'business in its social environment'.

S: Well, that still doesn't seem to be a radical change!

C: I think you're right. Some people say that Mr Jain, the Dean of Kellogg, has simply been doing a bit of marketing rebranding. You know, covering up any problems of the traditional MBA with a fashionable focus on 'social responsibility'. But maybe that's a bit unfair. Kellogg is still top of the rankings and sets the standards.

S: You mean Kellogg is one of the top schools – in terms of what? The number of job placements and starting salaries for its graduates?

C: Yes. The job market's got tougher for MBA graduates. But Mr Jain's efforts to find work for students compare very favourably with those of some of his counterparts. He's devoted a lot of his time to establishing and maintaining contacts with companies and potential employers. I've even heard that his staff struggle to keep up with the pace at which he travels the world building the 'Kellogg brand'. I was talking to one of the lecturers there the other day and he thought ...

Unit 2   **Leadership** page 8 (Track 4)

1   Many judgements have to be made on the basis of inaccurate information. Leaders often have to deal swiftly with conflicting demands without being sure of their facts. People who can't bear to cause pain or risk making enemies, or who need to be 100% sure before making up their minds, don't make good leaders.

2 Leading a large company, and dealing quickly with complicated and many-sided issues is a real challenge. Understanding the crucial point in complex situations is essential for devising an effective strategy. In order to survive demands on time and attention, a leader must be able to focus on what really matters.

3 A leader who can talk to all kinds of people – shareholders, the media, company employees, and so on, is essential. Motivating a large workforce requires an ability to present clear ideas and a clear vision persuasively. A leader who can't inspire trust will find the task difficult.

4 Well, Lord Stevenson, the chairman of the bank HBOS (and also of Pearson, which part-owns The Economist), says that he spends perhaps three-quarters of his time getting to know the top 150 people where he works. This shows that knowing who'll work best in which post is one of the key tasks of leadership.

5 People learn far more about leading from a good leader than from a great book. So, effective leaders need not only to see where the abilities of a particular individual would be best used; they also have to be teachers to those around them. That's the way to create leaders at many levels in an organisation.

6 As a leader you need an ability to work with people who may be better at their job than you are at some aspects of yours, but you still need to be able to guide and motivate them. Leaders who are jealous of their followers don't inspire loyalty. Successful leaders need to be able to say, 'I don't know what to do next,' without losing the respect of their colleagues.

Unit 3 Strategy page 12 (Track 5)

Good afternoon. Before I start my talk, I'd just like to thank Barton Business Forum for inviting me to speak this evening. The title of my talk is *The Importance of Strategic Planning*. I'm going to begin by looking at the importance of developing an effective strategy in business. I'm then going to go on to look at examples from different companies. If you have any questions, I'll be happy to answer them at the end. [PAUSE] So, let's get started. Developing an effective strategy is a key part of the planning process for all business organisations, and this is regardless of their size

and area of business. The first step is analysis. Analysing your strengths and weaknesses and where the business stands in relation to its markets and competitors enables you to identify potential opportunities for growth as well as potential threats. This process makes it possible for your organisation to set itself a number of strategic objectives. This brings me to my next point about the need to have clear objectives in order to plan resources.

Unit 4 Pay page 16 (Track 6)

L: Good morning everyone. I hope you've had a good week. Have you all had a chance to look at the handouts I gave you last Tuesday?

L: Good. OK, let's get started, shall we? As I said last week, today we'll be taking a critical look at CEOs and their pay packages. So, how does a company decide what level of pay to offer a new CEO? Well, a boss's remuneration is largely determined at the time of his or her appointment, which actually follows a fairly standard procedure. As soon as the CEO position becomes vacant, a selection committee tends to be appointed. And a recruitment consultant is usually invited in to help the committee. To determine what the new CEO's salary should be, consultants make use of benchmarks – looking at standards within the industry. They look at packages for executives at peer companies, that is, companies which are similar in terms of size and what they focus on. The question is whether this approach – and it is widespread – actually works.

S1: But doesn't that just mean that bosses' pay goes up and up?

L: Exactly! You see, no selection committee wants to award their new choice less than the industry average. For one thing, they think they won't be able to attract the best person to the job – and also, they believe it'll suggest that their company's settled for someone less than average. And that isn't all! You get further issues because the increase in pay doesn't seem to mean an increase in the time the new CEO stays in his or her job – their tenure. If you look at this slide for a moment – oh, it'd help if I had it the right way up – it shows the average tenure of top bosses over the last few years. As you can see, it's getting shorter and shorter, especially in Europe. In fact, a recent report from consultants at Booz Allen Hamilton showed that the turnover of top CEOs has almost tripled since 1995! So they're getting paid more for doing less for the companies they're appointed to!

L: But it's difficult to see who'll be brave enough to go against the benchmarking trend when it comes to deciding on remuneration. Having said that, a number of recent scandals over executive pay mean that some people are looking more closely at those who agreed to the contracts in the first place. But for the future of these businesses, what's needed is a major change – not a few reactions to scandals. So, what's the answer? Well, for a start, many people feel that if members of compensation committees were held more regularly accountable – I mean really held responsible – for the contracts they approve, then employees, shareholders and the general public might find that fewer CEO contracts were so shocking. Jo, I can see you want to say something.

S2:   I'm not sure I understand what you're saying about accountability. Are you saying that we need changes in the law ...?

Unit 5   Development page 20

Listening 1 (Track 7)

Thank you very much for inviting me to make this presentation about the World Bank Group. As I'm sure many of you already know, the World Bank is the world's leading development institution. The World Bank co-operates with governments, the private and public sectors and local groups. We work on projects in some of the poorest countries of the world – a situation which offers a number of challenges, as I'm sure you can imagine. Basically, we work towards poverty reduction and sustainable economic growth. We aim to raise standards by improving access to resources, and by sharing knowledge, building partnerships, and so on. For example, we develop loans to finance specific investments. We also offer policy advice.

Listening 2 (Track 8)

S: And for tonight's special report, business correspondent Luke Strong in our Birmingham studio looks at recent studies into economic growth in Brazil, Russia, India and China – otherwise known as the BRIC countries. Over to you, Luke.

L: Thank you, Siobhan. That's right. The economies of emerging countries are growing fast. Let's start by looking at China. Recent studies suggest that within half a century China's economy **is likely to overtake** that of any of the G7 countries: that is, America, Japan, Germany, France, Britain, Italy and Canada. In fact, most of the current G7 members **may not even continue** to be invited to attend meetings of the world's biggest economies!

And China isn't the only emerging economy developing in this way. A new study by Goldman Sachs compares the BRIC countries (remember, that's Brazil, Russia, India and China) with the G6. (Oh, by the way, the G6 leaves out Canada – since it accounts for only 3% of the G7's GDP.) Anyway, according to the study, the combined GDP of the BRIC countries is currently only one eighth of the output of the G6. But **it's expected that** the total output of the four BRIC economies **will overtake** that of the G6 in less than four decades, so by the middle of the century. And this **probably means that**, of today's G6, only America and Japan **will remain** among the world's six biggest economies by then. And in case you're wondering where these predictions come from, they're based on assumptions about population growth, the pace of investment, productivity growth, currency movements and that kind of thing.

If we just focus on specific dates, as mentioned in the report, it's thought that China **may well overtake** Germany by 2007, then Japan by 2015 and America by 2041. And India could **overtake** Japan by 2032.

Many people believe though that these kinds of long-term forecasts are **almost certainly going to be wrong** – not least because governments **may make** mistakes or political instability **may intervene**. Even so, it's generally considered to be a useful framework for understanding the rise of the emerging giants.

And now back to Siobhan in the studio for a round-up of today's news.

Unit 6   Marketing page 24 (Track 9)

So, how different are prices in Europe? Well, take whisky for example. A bottle of whisky costs almost 80% more in Amsterdam than in Rome.

But before Italians start celebrating, a packet of Nurofen headache pills is 70% dearer there than in Amsterdam. The creation of the euro in 1999 was supposed to encourage prices to converge, that is, to become more similar, by making it easier for people to compare prices in different countries. But this isn't quite what's happened. Although price gaps **did** narrow in the euro's first three years, an annual survey by Dresdner Kleinwort Wasserstein (DKW) has found no evidence of prices continuing to converge in the past two years.

DKW's survey covers the six biggest euro-area countries, and uses branded goods where possible, to allow like-for-like comparisons. It finds that Madrid has the cheapest total shopping basket, 10% less than in Paris – the most expensive city. If we consider for a moment individual prices, these differ by much more. Pampers nappies, for example, cost 56% more in Brussels than in Frankfurt. And a cinema ticket costs 170% more in Brussels than in Madrid. But Brussels is definitely the place for Levi jeans – 43% cheaper than in Paris in fact. The biggest price differences tend to be in non-tradable services. Branded electrical goods, such as irons and televisions, are easily shipped across borders, which is why they have the smallest price ranges. The euro should encourage prices to converge – not so much because consumers shop across borders, but because the ability to compare prices more easily encourages wholesalers to take advantage of price differences.

So why do prices still vary by so much? Well, there are at least three reasons. Firstly, the different tax rates, especially on alcohol. Secondly, national tastes – for example, bottled water, is still seen as a basic good in some countries, but a luxury in others – and finally, differences in the market structure. One big barrier is that there are still no large pan-European wholesalers or retailers, such as America's Wal-Mart. Leo Doyle, an economist at DKW, estimates that the price difference within the euro area is still roughly twice as large as in America. That suggests that there's still the opportunity for prices to come together.

The DKW survey also finds that, thanks to the rise in the euro, prices in London are no longer higher on average than in the euro area – in 2000 London was almost 20% more expensive than the euro-zone average. Britons still pay well over the top for their alcohol and cigarettes, but their country is cheaper by far the cheapest for books

and deodorants. Perhaps that's why so many of are concerned about joining the euro!

Unit 7   **Outsourcing** page 28 (Track 10)

F1: So, as I was saying, **I really think we should outsource our Customer Service division.** It would save us thousands of pounds – in terms of wages and general office overheads.

M1: **One way would be to set up a call centre,** in India say …

F1: India would be a good place, I agree … or the Philippines. Both countries provide large numbers of English speaking graduates …. and wages are certainly much lower there than they are here.

F2: Hmm … our clients are from all parts of Europe, particularly Germany. Will we also be able to get good German speakers?

M2: I've heard that there are already German-speaking call-centres in some countries – I'm not sure about India though. **Couldn't we** though **move closer to home,** to Eastern Europe, for example? Wages are relatively low there and it's certainly closer to our main markets.

F1: That's a good point, but I think wage differences are bound to be reduced over the next few years, so I'm not sure Eastern Europe is our answer. **Let's consider India again** – the people know our culture – which is important …

M2: But do you think a call centre in India could manage all the different types of calls we get?

M1: Well, perhaps for complex enquiries, where local understanding is vital, **what if we used people in the same country**? But for more routine back-office tasks and general enquiries, **how about shifting to India**?

F1: Good idea. I suggest we ask Sally to set up a meeting to discuss this further. Shall I draw up an agenda for the meeting?

Unit 8   **Finance** page 32 (Track 11)

F: And now over to John for an overview of the financial climate across Europe.

J: Thank you. Well, European factories continue to struggle. French industrial production decreased slightly during August, after falling by 1.8% in the previous 12 months. German industrial production also declined in the year to August, by 1.9%. But Italy's figures were more encouraging: although forecasts expected industrial output to decrease, it actually rose in August by 0.1%, following an increase of 1.7% in the previous 12 months. And in Sweden, industrial production rose by 3% in the year to August. Austria's economy grew by 0.7% in the year to the second quarter, compared with 0.8% in the year to the first quarter. And in Switzerland, retail sales plummeted by 3.2% in the year to August, while in Denmark they went up by the same rate. In Britain, the number of people claiming unemployment benefit fell in September to its lowest level since the mid-1970s, at 929,800 claimants. And wage growth rose to 3.4% in the 12 months to August, thanks mostly to higher public sector wages, which increased by 5.6%.

Unit 9 Recruitment page 36 (Track 12)

M: Hi Anne, Martin here. I just wanted to let you know I've got an interview for the management job I applied for with CTD.

A: **Really!**

M: **I know, I can hardly believe it myself,** especially as I sent the application form to the wrong address!

A: **You're kidding! How could you do a thing like that?**

M: I was addressing the envelope in a hurry and got mixed up. Luckily, I realised what I'd done and so I just rang up and asked the company for another form.

A: Yeah, but didn't they think it was strange?

M: Err ... I don't think so. I just told them the original form was ripped, and they sent me a new one straight away. **Oh, is that the time? I'm sorry, but I really have to go.** I've got to make a quick call about the job. **Anyway, why don't you ring me and maybe we could have lunch some time?**

A: **Sure. Good luck with the interview, by the way.**

M: Thanks, bye.

Unit 10 Counterfeiting page 40

Listening 1 (Track 13)
So, what happened in 2000? Well, a number of major record companies began merging with each other. This was because they assumed it would broaden their distribution and link music with other entertainment sales. For example, Warner Brothers and EMI tried – unsuccessfully at it happened – to join forces, and Vivendi became Vivendi Universal through acquisitions. At the time, sales of recorded music were peaking. They then fell by 5% in 2001 – and again by 9% in 2002. Record companies blame online file-swapping services for this. A court decision closed down Napster, the biggest file-swapping service, in September 2002, but smaller services had already started to replace it. Napster returned, though, as a pay service 13 months later. And another pay service, Apple's iTunes, has been extremely successful. The music industry still hasn't worked out whether it should allow consumers to copy music – or how to get them to start buying CDs again. Let's now speak to an expert on the music industry, Mike Fairfield. Mike, what do you think is the biggest challenge facing the music industry ...?

Listening 2 (Track 14)
F: Hello, Max?

M: Yes.

F: Hi, it's Jenny.

M: Hello there. What can I do for you?

F: I just wanted to let you know that I might be a bit late for this morning's team meeting.

M: No problem – and given that Jack's busy until 10 too, I suggest we just postpone the meeting until 12 so that we're all there.

F: Good idea. As I've got to go to the R & D Department anyway in a minute, I'll pop in and let Jack know on my way.

M: Thanks. See you later.

Unit 11 Markets page 44 (Track 15)

M: Hello Molly, Jason here.

F: Hi. I was just going to call you. **I was thinking we should** have a meeting to discuss the promotion for the latest perfume range with the whole sales team.

M: **How about getting** everyone together on Thursday?

F: **I'm afraid I can't** make Thursday myself, but Friday would be good.

M: OK. **I suggest we** invite Peter too, and ask him to bring along some of his photos. We'll need at least four for the website.

F: **Good idea. Maybe it would be worthwhile** inviting Sally along from the PR agency too. **We could do with** her advice on attracting customers better.

M: Well, **let's** keep our online discount? That seems to work OK, doesn't it?

F: **I don't know about** that. People come to our site once maybe, but they don't return to see what's new and to buy more.

M: Well, **why don't we** talk about it when we meet on Friday?

F: OK, I'll call Sally and Peter to see if they can make it and then send round an email to everyone to confirm times.

M: Thanks, Molly. Speak to you soon. Bye.

Unit 12   Lobbies page 48 (Track 16)

C: Good morning and welcome to Planet Life, where today we're discussing NGOs or Non-Governmental Organisations as many charities are described these days. **It's obvious that** governments and commercial companies need to be audited, that is checked by external organisations to ensure that their finances are in order. But **have you considered that** NGOs also need to be audited to ensure that they're being run efficiently? **We have to remember that** they're also human organisations – so we need to check against laziness, inefficiency and even corruption – as we do with any other organisation. That's why an organisation called Elephant Family has decided to audit the efforts of NGOs to preserve the Asian elephant. Let's hear what our environmental correspondent has to say about Elephant Family's work. Sally, ...

S: Thanks Cameron. Yes, well, **we all know about** the problems of wild African elephants, but Asia has its wild elephants too. However, unlike their African cousins, they mostly hide in forests, which is why so few people seem worried about what happens to them. Yet despite this, 21 NGOs in ten countries claim to be trying to preserve Asian elephants.

C: That seems a lot!

S: Yes, though only $4m a year is actually spent doing the work. I'm sure you'd agree though **that** $4m is still an amount of money worth auditing.

C: It certainly is!

S: Well, Elephant Family's audit report makes interesting reading. Firstly, they found that the best projects were run by local organisations rather than international ones.

C: Why's that? Because local enthusiasts are highly motivated?

S: That's right, Cameron. And the second interesting finding is that the larger NGOs aren't always effective. In fact, as the report itself puts it "Competition for funds and publicity among the larger NGOs results in a divided movement that is not making the best use of its resources". What's more, the report says that funds get moved from conservation to institutional survival and self-interest, resulting in a lack of transparency. In other words, money's sometimes spent on supporting the NGOs rather than preserving the animals they're intended to protect!

C: **Surely that means that** NGOS seriously need to re-evaluate the way they operate.

S: Yes, and that more questions may be asked in future about where funding is going. But it also means that some people may be unwilling to donate money to wildlife charities as they feel ...

Unit 13   Communication page 52

Listening 1 (Track 17)
The last thing companies want is to damage their reputation or image. So I think that when dealing with the media, there are a few key things they need to do. Firstly, it's crucial that companies always tell the truth. If there's a problem, they should say so straight away. I mean, they should admit it if they're at fault. But at the same time, they should stress the quick action they're taking to address the issue and to put things right. Basically, companies should try and find a way to turn any crisis into an opportunity. Um, and finally, I think it's a good idea to finish any interview on a positive note, like using a quote from someone from the company or giving information about an exciting new project the company's involved in – anything that will offer good PR really.

Listening 2 (Track 18)
I: Good morning. It's Midlands Weekly and Suzanne Jameson, Communications Manager at LWP, has joined us to discuss the effect of new technology on companies' communication. Welcome, Suzanne.

S: Thank you.

I: Let's start with the internet and intranets. They seem the perfect way for companies to communicate – but is this the case?

S: Well, as workers in some companies become more geographically separated, often as a result of cost-cutting measures where operations move to cheaper areas, managers need a way to boost staff morale and build a corporate culture, that is, get employees to feel part of the same team wherever they are and teach them to understand the core qualities of the business.

I: And this is where intranets have a major role?

S: Exactly. In some companies, certain staff rarely come into the office. For example, a quarter of IBM's workforce is mobile, spending over 80% of their time off-site, working from home or on the road. Key people might even be based in markets abroad, a day's air travel away from head office.

I: That's true. And things are changing faster and faster these days, so I imagine a company intranet allows you to explain to employees what's happening, and why.

S: Exactly. It allows companies to ensure that every employee shares the same corporate news, views and vision. Some use it to teach employees (and suppliers and customers) their ethical code, like the policy on accepting free gifts from suppliers. Boeing, for instance, offers an online 'ethics challenge'.

I: So what other uses are made of company intranets?

S: Well, another key use is that bosses tell staff the direction they want the company to go in. For example, at Ford, which claims to have the world's largest intranet, 170,000 staff around the world are emailed a weekly note from Jac Nasser, the CEO. A purpose-built newsroom there maintains a website that's upgraded several times a day, and is available in English to Ford's employees around the world, as well as to staff at its new acquisitions such as Volvo.

I: Aha. Suzanne, we've been speaking about the **benefits** of new technology, particularly company intranets. Are there any negative effects?

S: Oh yes. All this communication from on high can certainly cause problems. At SAP, the German business-software giant, for example, they found that some middle managers objected to the Chairman emailing all employees. You see, their authority had rested partly on their role as a source of information, and without it they felt undermined or threatened. So what appeared to be a simple, time-saving innovation turned out to be more complex and politically sensitive.

I: I see.

S: And there might be some sensitivity as communications become increasingly bottom-up as well as top-down. The Chief Information Officer at Siemens, a person called Chittur Ramakrishnan, for example, has noticed a significant number of emails going directly to top management. The idea of going through a secretary has altered. People can send emails to anyone and expect a response. It's all very democratising.

I: So it sounds. Suzanne, I'm afraid we're going to have to stop there. Thank you for joining us today.

M: You're welcome.

Unit 14   Logistics page 56

Listening 1 (Track 19)

1 What kind of employee would you say you are?

2 How do you react to criticism?

3 What developments do you expect to see in your business over the next 5 years?

4 Why have you decided to leave your job?

5 How did you contribute to the success of your last company?

6 What kind of remuneration package are you looking for?

7 Where do you see yourself in 10 years' time?

8 Do you consider yourself to be a good team player?

Listening 2 (Track 20)

Hello. This is Melanie Reilly, that's R-E-I-DOUBLE L-Y – calling from Kell Ltd. Er ... I just wanted to thank you for sending your catalogue. We're interested in stocking one of your new bicycle ranges in our stores – that's catalogue number OU390. So, er, could you please send us price details for 50 of these, as well as your payment and delivery terms. The address is 76 High Street, Minton, MI10 8RT. Thank you. Er, goodbye.

So what do we know about successful innovations – and also about innovations that fail? Well, a very good explanation of this can be found in an interesting study by three academics: Lehmann, Goldenberg and Mazursky. In their study they looked at 197 product innovations. Of these, 111 were successes and 86 failures. What they found was that the successful innovations had some, or all, of a set of common features. They were moderately new to the market and based on tried and tested technology. Basically, they supported existing practices. Also, they met customers' needs and saved money. Those are the successful innovations. By contrast, the products that failed were based on cutting-edge – or untested – technology. Also, they were created with no clearly defined solution in mind. And they followed on from other people's work.

So, it's interesting, isn't it, that we're not talking about totally revolutionary products when we're thinking about successful innovation. What we're talking about is a new way of looking at things to meet a real need.

And that brings me on to news of an event organised by *The Economist*. Later this month, they'll be hosting a day-long discussion on the factors that promote successful innovation inside some organisations but not in others. And that'll be followed by the announcement of the winners of *The Economist*'s Innovation Awards for this year. The idea is to celebrate and thank a handful of individuals who through innovations in their chosen technological fields, have been successful at creating new economic and intellectual wealth for the rest of us to enjoy.

BEC Vantage practice test

Listening Test Part One (Conversation 1)
(Track 22)

M: ALX Recruitment.

F: Hello, this is Janet Byers from HR at PRO Limited.

M: Oh, hello, Janet. It's David. How can I help you today?

F: Oh, hi, David. We're looking for a Team Leader and were hoping you could help.

M: We'll certainly do our best. Is this for the Sales Department again?

F: Actually, it's for Customer Services.

M: Right. Is it a permanent position?

F: No, just for 4 months over the summer period.

M: I see. And the ideal starting date?

F: Well, the current member of staff was going to leave on the 3rd April, but can stay now until the end of the month. So if we said the 1st of May, that'd be great.

M: OK. Does the new person need any particular qualifications or skills?

F: They'd need to have a diploma or a degree but the subject isn't important. They'll be liaising with all kinds of clients and staff so the key thing is communication. They need excellent abilities in that area. Some kind of management background would also help – but it's not essential.

R Fine. And what were you thinking of in terms of salary?

Listening Test Part One (Conversation 2)
(Track 23)

F: Hello, Howard? It's Sharon. Did you listen to the business news this morning?

M: No, what's happened?

F: The top story was that Norcom has fired Oscar Case.

M: The Chairman?

F: No, that's Sam Killian. I'm talking about the Chief Executive.

M: What for? It must be something major.

F: Well, it seems there's been a lengthy investigation that's apparently revealed that he was directly involved in fraudulent accounting practices at the company. And, as you know, Norcom is responsible for our complete telecommunications system!

M: Yes, but maybe their problems won't actually affect us. We need a meeting about this though, don't we? We need to ensure we're all aware of the potential risks and what to do about them.

F: That's right. Could you organise that, do you think? We'll also need to appoint a key member of staff to report to the board about any issues related to Norcom.

M: OK, I'll start to look into that. I'll be in touch again soon.

Listening Test Part One (Conversation 3)
(Track 24)

Hello, this is Chris Macintyre – that's M-A-C-I-N-T-Y-R-E – from Mistral Limited, calling at 3 pm on

Thursday the 10th. I'd like to leave a message for Simon Marks. Um, Simon, I really just wanted to let you know that Peter Carr passed on the latest comments you made about the business plans. They're really useful – so many thanks for those! Oh, and by the way, Peter mentioned to me that he invited you to join us at the meeting on Tuesday. One of the things we're going to discuss there is our current promotional strategy. That's because something's not really going right regarding sales and advertising and we seem to be having trouble drawing in enough customers. I hope you can come. Anyway, perhaps you could call and let me know if you can make the meeting or not. My extensions's 324. Er, thanks, goodbye.

Listening Test Part Two (Section 1)
(Track 25)

13   Although I'm sure many people would disagree with me, in my opinion, buyers won't always look for the lowest price when they're making a purchase. Other factors like image or convenience may be just as important. For me, the key thing is getting quality goods that are worth what you pay for them. I really think most people do actually expect products to meet minimum standards in terms of quality.

14   I'd say that buyers feel happier buying from a reliable firm than one they hardly know. This means choosing a company with a record of selling quality products. In practice, it usually means one that's demonstrated solid financial performance – preferably for some time. Buyers, including me, don't want to be let down. The old saying 'Nobody ever got fired for buying IBM' still applies. Or at least that's what I think.

15   Lack of availability of goods or delivery of damaged items that finally arrive days after you've ordered them can really damage a company's good name. It's not surprising really, when you think how important these issues are to customers like me. For many companies, the need to get things to the customer quickly is crucial. And even with direct sales and the internet, there still need to be smooth systems in place for getting the product to the customer.

16   I know from experience that things like lost orders, inaccurate invoices and poor correspondence don't impress clients. People expect to be treated well – from the way their initial enquiry, order or complaint is dealt with, right through to a quick phone call to check that any problems have been sorted out. In a number of companies, like the one I work for, this type of thing is viewed as a strategic activity, with dedicated staff and documented procedures.

17   I'd say the level of support offered is really critical for many products. For complex technical products, this might even be the most important factor when a customer's determining whether to go ahead and buy or not. If they can't ring for help 24 hours a day, many people will simply decide to go elsewhere. I personally think there's no point in paying out a lot of money unless you feel secure about using it in the future.

Listening Test Part Two (Section 2)
(Track 26)

18   Hello and thank you all for being here. Many of you will have heard the rumours of takeover bids, plant closures and so on. Well, I'm here today to tell you that while we will be joining MKL, the global retailer, this won't result in any immediate redundancies here in Marston. The plan is for the companies to unite as equals, building on the strengths that each firm has to offer. Does anyone have any questions at this stage?

19   After suffering from disappointing sales last year, I'm happy to confirm that we've had a much better start to the year financially and to say that things are looking up. I know there was bitterness about our inability to increase salaries last year – but I'm glad to be able to let you know that as we predicted, we're now in a position to add the 3% we discussed to monthly pay packets. This will take effect from April this year.

20   And to finish, I'd like to share with you some important news. Today Briston Production has been in the business headlines. Improvements in efficiency mean that we've made more money in the last 12 months than ever before. And it's all down to your hard work. In order to show the company's appreciation, you'll all receive a bonus this month. So thank you very much again for your commitment to the company. And thank you for your attention.

21   Staff are currently entitled to take leave when they wish – provided they give at least three days' notice to their immediate line manager. To bring us in line with other companies in the PTM group, staff will now be expected to complete a leave request form

for their line manager to sign. This then goes to Personnel for formal approval. The whole process could take two weeks, so it's important to get the form filled in as soon as possible.

22 Can I start by confirming rumours of expansion to the Hetby site. Following the launch of the CV3 in Asia, we're unlikely to meet all new orders using the existing production facility. The planned expansion will create over 50 new posts and offer promotion opportunities for many existing staff. If anyone's interested in working in a supervisory capacity in the new factory, please get in touch with HR. Details of the new facility will be appearing in the press shortly.

Listening Test Part 3 (Track 27)

F: Welcome to *Business World*. A revolution's taking place in the world of business and it's called employee power. Hundreds of employees have already taken part in employee buyouts, buying the company they work for, and the numbers are rising. So, is this the company of the future? With me in the studio today I have Tony Vanetti. Tony's gone back to university to study employee power. Hello, Tony.

M: Hello, Rebecca.

F: Well, Tony, the big news this year is that there's been an employee buyout at the Scottish fish company, Highlander. What were reactions to the buyout, Tony?

M: Well, Highlander's a very respected company and there had been fears that it would be bought out by a bank or investment company and that the assets would be sold off with no concern for the local area. So clients were very relieved that this didn't happen. Indeed, the retail side of the business – the chain of fish restaurants – has increased sales by 8% since the buyout – in a year that hasn't been kind to tourism.

F: So is Highlander planning to open new restaurants?

M: That's unlikely in the short term – though it is seeking to acquire further suppliers – or so I've been led to believe. An employee-run firm that has opened new outlets recently, though, is the Muscovy Partnership, the supermarket chain. And last week, against the trend, it announced a 130 millon pound refurbishment programme for all its outlets.

F: Umm, it's the best known example of employee participation in the UK, isn't it?

M: That's right. It's got more than 50,000 partners, who are all called to vote on aspects of development of the firm, from changes in store openings to investment policy. It's a shame more companies don't ask workers their views on strategic decisions in this way.

F: Absolutely. Moving on to your research, you've come across some surprising facts about employee participation, haven't you?

M: Yes. A number of these facts are about companies' attitudes to partnerships. According to a study undertaken by Western Bank, for example, firms owned by their employees are a better lending risk. You might have thought the opposite would be true.

F: And there are wider benefits too, aren't there?

M: Yes. In my thesis, I focused on three towns in Italy with a higher than average proportion of worker co-operatives. I found that the workers were healthier than in other towns, there was less crime, and there's more community involvement in educational and social affairs.

F: Interesting! Tony, your interest in co-operatives actually arose because of personal involvement, didn't it? I believe you took control of the failing paper-making business owned by your family and within nine years you'd sold it to the thousand employees of the company.

M: That's right. Things started to improve when I took over. But the increase in productivity once the employees had taken a share in it was astonishing. I'd expected the main reason for this to be the increased sense of self-esteem or the fact that people felt that they were earning money directly for themselves rather than making someone else rich. It turned out, though, that the key thing they spoke about was simpler: the greater choice about working hours. I'm still involved as a non-executive director – so it's interesting to keep up with the changes that have occurred there.

F: That's very interesting, Tony. We're now going to take a short break. After the break we're going to look at further findings about worker co-operatives and how working conditions …

Answer key

Unit 1 | Companies

Vocabulary (page 4)
Ex 1: 2 customer 3 merger 4 entrepreneur
5 bureaucratic 6 network 7 hierarchical 8 shareholder
9 supplier
Ex 2: 2 of 3 for 4 to 5 to 6 to 7 with 8 of 9 by/with
10 with

Listening 1 (page 5)
Ex 1: 2 Type of company: Small and medium-sized
enterprises **Type of student:** One or two key members of
staff sponsored
3 Type of company: Start-up companies **Type of
student:** Boss/founder of the company might fund his/her
own studies
Ex 2: customer services, finance, human resources,
production, administration
Ex 3: marketing, sales, logistics, IT, procurement, legal
services etc.

Listening 2 (page 5)
Ex 1: Challenges facing Kellogg: Maybe a reaction
against a management elite after corporate scandals in
recent years. Maybe because of a gap between what
graduates of business schools can offer and what
companies actually need.
Changes to courses at Kellogg: Allowing students to
specialise sooner, hopefully making them more useful to
employers. A class on 'leadership in times of crisis', which
used to be optional, is now mandatory. A few new courses,
e.g. ethics and business in its social environment.
Other changes at Kellogg: Some people say that Kellogg
has been doing a bit of marketing rebranding, covering up
any problems of the traditional MBA with a fashionable
focus on social responsibility. The Dean, Mr Jain, has
devoted time to establishing and maintaining contacts
with companies and potential employers, building the
'Kellogg brand'.
Ex 2: 2e 3a 4c 5d 6f

Reading (page 6)
Ex 1: 2e 3d 4f 5c 6a

Language check (page 7)
Ex 1: 2f 3a 4e 5d 6c
Ex 2: 2 is 3 're currently having 4 know 5 think 6 usually
see 7 understand 8 don't work 9 imagine 10 looks
11 'm attending 12 is going

Writing (page 7) Suggested answer (50 words)
Sam
Sorry but I can't make it on Monday 23 May as I'm visiting
an external supplier and I'm not coming back until the
Friday. How about Monday 30 May? If you're free then, we
could meet at 10 o'clock. Shall I book a room?
Regards
Sam

Unit 2 | Leadership

Vocabulary (pages 8 and 9)
Ex 1: 2 deadline 3 delegate 4 dominate 5 valued
6 inspire

Ex 2: 2 of 3 on 4 into 5 on 6 to 7 by/with 8 to 9 in
10 to
Ex 3: 2e 3a 4c 5d 6f
Ex 4: 2 attend 3 set 4 resolve 5 take 6 found
Ex 5: 3d 4a 5d 6c 7a 8b. The following test verb & noun
combinations: 2, 5 and 8.
Ex 6: 2 Take 3 give 4 Don't set 5 make 6 Develop
7 Don't lose 8 Avoid 9 Create 10 don't dominate

Language check (page 10)
2 Gabi Hart is a director.
3 A manager is not the same as a leader.
4 Employees don't want to be led; they want to be
managed. CORRECT
5 Does fear really motivate people to do better in their
work?
6 Most managers learn from experience.
7 Bob is one of the youngest managers here but he's also
one of the best.
8 Culture can affect attitudes to management. CORRECT
9 The newspaper article I read on the train this morning
was very positive about management today.
10 I don't know of many really strong leaders in the world
at the moment. CORRECT

Listening (page 10)
Ex 1: 2d 3f 4e 5a 6b
Ex 2: 2 complex 3 effective 4 conflicting 5 jealous
6 crucial

Writing (page 11)
Ex 1: choosing, importance, where, chief, successfully, least,
lots/a lot, four, decision, which, business
Ex 2: Suggested answer
Would you do me a favour?

Dear Mike
I'm going to be at a conference for the rest of the week.
Would you do me a favour and deal with a few things for
me while I'm away? Would you mind asking Jason Black to
leave his report on my desk for when I get back? Also, I'd
really appreciate it if you could also let the sales team
know tomorrow's meeting has been postponed until next
Wednesday.
Thanks
Franz

Unit 3 | Strategy

Reading (pages 12 and 13)
Ex 1: Current sectors of activity: scent, cosmetics,
spectacles, watches, accessories, furniture, flowers,
chocolate, sweets, jam, marmalade, cafés, restaurants, night
clubs
Proposed new sector: hotels
Advantages: A strong product and a strong experience at
the hotel can combine to create a super-brand; positive
publicity
Risks: Potential loss of control and brand dilution if
quality is not appropriate
Ex 2: 2 Bulgari (jeweller): Joint venture with Ritz-Carlton to
build hotels and resorts
3 Salvatore Ferragamo (shoemaker): Designed hotels in
Florence

4 Pierre Cardin (luxury goods): Lost good name by giving out licences all over the world that did not deliver appropriate quality
5 Yves St Laurent (luxury goods): Lost good name by giving out licences all over the world that did not deliver appropriate quality
6 Christian Dior (luxury goods): Lost good name by giving out licences all over the world that did not deliver appropriate quality
7 Calvin Klein (luxury goods): Lost control of distribution of products in many countries
Ex 3: 2g 3h 4a 5f 6c 7d 8e

Writing (page 14) Suggested answer (44 words)
Dear Mr Jacobs
I would be delighted to speak at your business forum on 3rd July. The title of my presentation will be 'The importance of successful strategic planning'. Please could I have access to a video and overhead projector?
Yours sincerely
Lynne Davis

Listening (page 14)
Ex 1: The phrases from the audioscript are in bold.
2 before I start my talk, I'd just like to thank ...
3 this brings me to my next point
4 I hope you have found my comments useful
5 if you have any questions, I'll be happy to answer them at the end
6 on this next slide, you can see ...
Ex 2: 2 potential 3 growth 4 threats 5 analysis
6 enables 7 opportunities 8 key 9 effective
10 competitors

Language check (page 15)
Ex 1: 2 're holding 3 'll be 4 will meet 5 'll call
6 leaves 7 'm going to begin 8 are you doing
9 aren't going to have 10 'll come
Ex 2: 2 'm seeing/'m going to see 3 're having/'re going to have 4 starts/will start/is going to start 5 won't finish/isn't going to finish 6 won't be able to/'m not going to be able to 7 are you doing 8 'm giving
9 'll be/'m going to be 10 gets/will get/is going to get
11 'll phone

Vocabulary (page 15)
2 an opportunity 3 an objective 4 resources
5 customers

Unit 4   Pay

Reading (page 16)
Ex 1: total compensation, pension fund, perk, company loan ('forgiven' on departure), shares, restricted stock
Ex 2: 2 the median (average) total compensation of the CEOs
3 the limit of shares Trevor Fetter could buy
4 the amount American Airline's bosses put into a protected pension fund
5 the length of time Charles Conaway had been in his job
6 the amount of the company loan given to Charles Conaway and cancelled when he left

Vocabulary (page 17)
Ex 1: 2e 3f 4a 5c 6g 7d
Ex 2 : 2b 3c 4a 5d 6c 7a 8b 9d 10d

Listening (page 18)
Ex 1: 2 consultants make use of benchmarks, comparing with similar companies within the industry and making salary decisions on that basis.

3 bosses' salaries go up and up.
4 the turnover of top CEOs has almost tripled since 1995.
5 members of compensation committees were more accountable for the appointments they make.
Ex 2: vacancy, golden hello

Writing (page 18)
Suggested answer
Position vacant: Area sales manager (Sheffield)
We offer:
– An above-average base salary
– An annual bonus linked to performance
– A generous pension
– Excellent working conditions
To apply, email: jane2@TER _recruitment.com

Language check (page 19)
Ex 1: 2 down 3 up 4 down 5 off 6 up
Ex 2: 2 It has not been as easy as expected.
3 We managed to catch up in the final month.
4 They have run into a problem.
5 I am not sure I will meet the deadline.
6 We were behind schedule throughout the project.
Ex 3: 2 stepped 3 did not want 4 directed 5 has not yet been 6 sacked 7 have already come 8 have awarded 9 burst 10 rose 11 fell 12 have led to 13 received 14 dropped 15 threatened 16 resigned

Unit 5   Development

Vocabulary (page 20)
Ex 1: 2d 3d 4c 5b 6a
Ex 2: 2h 3f 4a 5c 6d 7e 8g
Ex 3: 2e 3d 4a 5f 6c

Listening 1 (page 21)
Ex 1: 2 governments, private and public sectors, local groups 3 poor countries 4 to reduce poverty, achieve sustainable economic growth, raise standards

Ex 2: Suggested answers
2 it's the world's leading development institution.
3 governments, the private and public sectors and local groups.
4 projects in some of the poorest countries of the world.
5 reduce poverty, achieve sustainable economic growth, raise standards by improving access to resources
6 develop loans to finance specific investments and also offer policy advice.
Ex 3: access (SAME), project (verb)/project (noun) (DIFFERENT), aim (SAME), challenge (SAME)

Reading (page 21)
1 for 2 a 3 as 4 than 5 about 6 CORRECT 7 CORRECT 8 and 9 the 10 them

Language check (page 22)
Ex 1: 2 in 3 to 4 on 5 to 6 of 7 on 8 in
Ex 2: Certainty: is going to, would (as a consequence of another action), must (used to express the speaker's view)
Probability: should **Possibility:** may, might, could

Listening 2 (page 22)
Ex 1 and Ex 2:
BRIC: India, China
G7: Japan, France, Britain, Italy and Canada
Ex 3: 2 false 3 false 4 true
Ex 4: See audioscript on page 82.
Ex 5: 2d 3e 4a 5c

Writing (page 23)
Ex 1: Suggested answers
2 The UK's economic growth should stay strong this year.
3 GDP per capita in the UK is likely to keep well above average compared with the new entrants to the EU.
4 The housing market in the UK may continue to be extremely active.
5 The UK might never recover its position as one of the world's top industrial nations.
Ex 2: 2 roads 3 supplies 4 damage 5 know-how 6 data 7 advice 8 revenue
Ex 3: Suggested answer (56 words)

Dear Sir/Madam
I saw your advertisement for consultants for Helix International in World Today magazine and am very interested in learning more about the positions. I would be grateful if you could send an information pack to me at the following address:
14b Stanley Terrace
Peterley
PT2 8TY.
Thank you very much.
Yours faithfully
Lorna Markley

Unit 6   Marketing

Listening (page 24)
Ex 1: 1 It uses branded goods where possible to allow like-for-like comparisons.
2 whisky, alcohol, headache pills, nappies, cinema tickets, irons, televisions, bottled water, cigarettes, books, deodorants
3 different tax rates, especially on alcohol, national tastes, differences in market structure
Ex 2: 2 false 3 true 4 false 5 false 6 true 7 false 8 true

Language check (page 24)
2 than 3 least 4 best 5 most 6 happiest 7 generous 8 equal

Vocabulary (pages 25 and 26)
Ex 1: 2d 3c 4a 5c
Ex 2: 2b 3c 4a 5b 6a 7c 8a
Ex 3: 2 to 3 into 4 on 5 to 6 of 7 up 8 on
Ex 4: 2 consistent 3 ambition 4 reliable 5 competitive 6 responsible 7 security 8 cynical 9 evil 10 valuable

Writing (page 26)
Ex 1: 2 organisation 3 successful 4 qualification 5 analysis 6 advertising 7 creative 8 extending
Ex 2: Suggested answer (76 words)

Dear Makki
This is just to let you know that we've decided to offer the Marketing Manager job to Heikki Joensu. Both candidates seem very capable. However, although the other candidate, Pirjo Hakkonen, is significantly more qualified than Heikki, she's a lot less experienced. She also asked for much more money than we can offer. We think Heikki Joensu will do an excellent job and will fit in well with his colleagues here.
Best wishes
Louis

Reading (page 27)
Ex 1: Growth in The Economist's client base, increased brand awareness, increase in revenue
3 If your assistant reads The Economist, don't play too much golf. Given a choice, would you pick your brain?

Ex 2: 2c 3a 4e 5d 6g 7f 8i 9j 10h
2 interests 3 campaign 4 client 5 awareness 6 advertising 7 make 8 position 9 market 10 adopt

Unit 7   Outsourcing

Vocabulary (page 28)
Ex 1: 2 f 3 a 4 g 5 h 6 e 7 d 8 c
Ex 2: 2a 3b 4b 5c 6a 7c 8b 9c 10b

Reading (pages 29 and 30)
Ex 1: Companies in higher cost countries: easyGroup, Thames Water, United Utilities, Sainsbury, BT, BA, P&O, National Grid, Barclays, Prudential and others in finance, National Health Service
Contractors in lower cost countries: Tata Consultancy Services (TCS), Infosys
Potential benefits to higher cost countries: competitive advantage through cost saving, potentially better solutions
Potential benefits to lower cost countries: foreign revenue
Ex 2: 2 potential size of the increase in revenue for India from BPO this year
3 Britain's contribution in jobs to outsourcing to India this year
4 the price charged per minute per phone call for customers
5 typical call centre savings following offshoring
6 combined turnover in 2003–4 of the top three Indian IT outsourcing companies
7 percentage of Wipro's business with Britain
8 Britain's proportion of the western European economy
Ex 3: 2 rival 3 abroad 4 rise 5 the equivalent of 6 handling 7 imprecise 8 solutions 9 turnover 10 trade
Ex 4: 2 reduce/reduction 3 lose/loss 4 redundant/redundancy 5 laid off/lay off
Ex 5: 2 redundant 3 redundancies/layoffs 4 laid 5 cuts/losses 6 to reduce/to cut

Language check (page 31)
2 If we advertised …
3 … if we moved …
4 If I were you, …
5 We might be better off if we consult /consulted …
6 If we reduce …
7 If we don't get …, we'll have to …
8 I suggest employing …

Listening (page 31)
Ex 1: 1 Setting up a call centre in India or the Philippines or in Eastern Europe
2 Have a meeting to discuss the matter further. The proposal is to use people in the home country for complex enquiries where local knowledge is vital, and to outsource routine back office tasks and general enquiries to India.
Ex 2: See audioscript on page 84.

Writing (page 31)
Suggested answer

Dear Elena
We think we should outsource our Customer Service division to somewhere like India. If we did this, we could cut our costs, particularly in terms of overheads, by as much as 50%. It would also enable the staff here to concentrate on more complex business processes.
We have asked Sally to arrange a meeting for us to discuss

this within the next two weeks. Could you suggest any dates that would suit you?
Best wishes
Marc

Unit 8   Finance

Listening (page 32)
Ex 1: (n) indicates that the same form is also used for the noun. Verbs in italics are mentioned in Ex 2.
Upward trend: *go up, rise* (n), *increase* (n), soar, jump (n), skyrocket
Downward trend: go down, *decline* (n), drop (n), *decrease* (n), *fall* (n), plunge (n), *plummet*, nosedive (n), slide (n), dip (n)
Ex 2: 2d 3c 4a

Language check (pages 32 and 33)
Ex 1: 1 has 2 the 3 more 4 CORRECT 5 CORRECT 6 up 7 slight 8 such 9 CORRECT 10 of
Ex 2: 1 Share prices have fallen very quickly.
2 The company has been extremely slow to cut costs.
3 Company performance is expected to improve steadily over the year.
4 Following the takeover, the future looks positive for MNP.
Ex 3: 2 you will notice that
3 let's move on to the next slide
4 the graph clearly shows
5 this has led to the trend you see here
Ex 4: 2 The graph clearly shows
3 you will notice that
4 has led to the trend you see here
5 let's move on to the next slide
Ex 5: 1 The percentage of people receiving health insurance from their employers fell from 62.6% to 61.3% in 2002.
2 In 2002, the number of Americans without health insurance rose by 5.7% to 43.6m.
3 1.7m more people fell below the poverty line between 2000 and 2002. This meant that there was an increase in the poverty rate of 4%, from 11.7% to 12.1%.

Vocabulary (page 34)
Ex 1: 2a 3d 4c 5g 6h 7e 8f

Reading (page 34)
Ex 1: 2l 3a 4g 5f 6c 7h 8i 9k 10d 11e 12 j
Ex 2: 2 The executives received Skr 550m more in bonus payments than they told shareholders about; the former CEO, Petersson, removed the limit on one of the two bonus schemes; in another transaction Petersson and his deputy received Skr 70m more than authorised; executives took – and renovated – corporate flats for themselves and their families.
3 Because the share price has fallen to one-tenth of its peak.
4 It successfully moved into the American market in the 1990s but had to sell the company in December 2002 when it started making losses.
5 Positive – the company is basically sound and the new bosses are changing the company for the better.

Writing (page 35) Suggested answer (94 words)
During the late 1990s Skandia was a favourite of investors. Its share price soared from 50 Skr in 1999 to Skr 225 in June 2000. However, over the next two years the company suffered from the stockmarket crash and the misbehaviour of its top managers. By the end of 2002, its share price had plummeted to Skr 20, only one tenth of its peak, and the

company was forced to sell American Skandia. Over the next 12 months, as rumours of a takeover bid continued, Skandia's share price remained steady at around Skr 25.

Unit 9   Recruitment

Vocabulary (pages 36 and 37)
Ex 1:

c	t	G	R	A	D	U	A	T	E
A	C	C	E	P	T	A	N	C	E
n	t	m	e	s	e	r	s	H	m
d	a	n	c	y	s	a	e	E	s
i	O	F	F	E	R	t	l	C	c
d	z	x	b	n	m	i	e	K	r
A	D	V	E	R	T	n	c	s	e
t	t	H	I	R	E	g	t	a	e
e	t	P	O	S	I	T	I	O	N
k	I	N	T	E	R	V	I	E	W

Ex 2: 2b 3e 4b 5a 6d
Ex 3: 2c 3a 4e 5f 6d
Ex 4: 2 cover letter 3 background 4 small talk 5 database 6 payroll
Ex 5: 2 in 3 for 4 from 5 to 6 for
Ex 6: 2 requirement 3 qualify
4 advertising/advertisement 5 select 6 notify
7 application 8 recruitment 9 specify 10 acceptance

Language check (page 38)
Ex 1: 2 whose 3 who 4 that 5 that 6 who 7 which 8 whom
It is possible to delete the relative pronoun from sentences 4 and 7 because it refers to the object of the verb.
Ex 2: 2 I guess I'd better be going 3 Would you excuse me? 4 Nice meeting you 5 I don't want to keep you any longer 6 Why don't you give me a call? 7 Great talking to you 8 See you sometime soon 9 What exactly do you mean by that? 10 I didn't realise it was so late

Listening (page 38)
Ex 1: 2a 3c 4e 5h 6b 7d 8f 9i
Ex 2: Small talk phrases are shown in bold in the audioscript on page 84.

Writing (page 39)
Ex 1: See suggested answer in corrected version of Ex 2 below.
Ex 2:
Dear Mr Walker
I am writing to apply for the position of Office Manager as advertised on the CTEL web site.
As you can see from the attached CV, I am an experienced Office Manager. I have managed 35 staff at RRT Limited for four years. I also have a Degree in Management Studies from Manchester University and a Diploma in French from Lancaster College.
I enjoy the challenge of running a busy office and consider myself to be resourceful, sociable, well-organised and calm in a crisis.
If you have any questions, please do not hesitate to contact me. I look forward to hearing from you.
Yours sincerely
Kate Glad

Unit 10   Counterfeiting

Vocabulary (page 40)
2e 3i 4g 5c 6h 7d 8a 9j 10f
Listening
Ex 1: Warner Brothers, EMI, Vivendi, Napster, iTunes.
Napster and iTunes are online music services.
Ex 2: 2 false 3 false 4 false 5 true
Ex 3: 2 acquisition 3 entertainment 4 replace 5 sales
6 merge
Reading (page 41)
1b 2c 3a 4a 5c
Language check (page 42)
2 If you continue 3 CORRECT 4 CORRECT
5 more foreigners would visit 6 If I were you, I'd take
7 I wouldn't have reported 8 CORRECT
Listening 2 (page 42)
Ex 1: 2 They postpone the meeting until 12.
3 to let Jack know about the meeting while she's in the
R&D Department
Ex 2: Words and phrases in the tapescript: given, so
that, as
Other words and phrases: because, since, due to, in
view of, the reason ... is to, in order to, so, so as to
Ex 3: Suggested answers
1 to go to the doctor's. 2 that everything's so urgent.
3 to attend a conference. 4 to recruitment difficulties.
5 I can give you a hand if you like.
Writing (page 42) Suggested answer (35 words)
Mike
As I've got half an hour before our meeting, I'm just going
to see Molly so that I can explain the problems we're
having with the software in person. I'll be back soon.
Laura
Reading 2 (page 43)
Ex 1: Fighting counterfeit products
Ex 2: 2 fake 3 victims 4 enforcing 5 law 6 goods
7 copied 8 legal 9 shoddy 10 infringing
11 manufactured 12 software 13 affected 14 courts
15 pirate

Unit 11   Markets

Vocabulary (page 44)
Ex 1: 2f 3h 4c 5d 6a 7e 8g
Ex 2: 2 advertisement 3 auction 4 supply/supplier
5 demand 6 discussion
Ex 3: 2d 3c 4c 5d 6b 7b 8d
Reading 1 (page 45)
Ex 1: 2 false 3 false 4 false 5 true 6 false
Ex 2: 2 buyers 3 transaction 4 income
5 acquisition 6 sales 7 risks 8 monopoly
9 interest 10 investigation
Language check (page 45)
2 to set 3 to speak 4 to invest 5 ignoring
6 evaluating 7 Building 8 to take over
9 to negotiate 10 to meet
Reading 2 (page 46)
Ex 1: 2c 3d 4e 5a 6c 7d
Ex 2: 2d 3e 4c 5f 6a
Listening (page 47)
Ex 1: 2 photos 3 PR agency 4 online discount
Ex 2: See phrases for making/responding to suggestions in

bold in the audioscript on page 84. See page 98 of the
coursebook for further phrases.
Writing (page 47) Suggested answer (75 words)
Dear all
There will be a meeting at 10.00 on Friday 3 March in
Meeting Room 2 to discuss the online promotion for the
new perfume range. Let's start by discussing how we can
get customers' attention and arouse interest. We should
also consider what kind of promotional offers would be
suitable. In addition, I suggest we discuss different ways of
encouraging repeat visits to the website.
I look forward to seeing you on the 3rd.
Best wishes
Molly

Unit 12   Lobbies

Vocabulary (pages 48 and 49)
Ex 1: People and organisations: activist, campaigner,
NGO (non-governmental organisation), celebrity, pressure
group
Issues: duty, aid, imports, environment, subsidies, quotas,
fair trade, tariff barriers
Action: boycott, sit-in, demonstration, petition, march,
letter of protest
Ex 2: 2 of 3 with 4 against 5 in 6 of 7 to 8 at
Ex 3: 2c 3b 4c 5a 6c 7b 8b
Ex 4: 2 generate 3 take 4 make 5 raise 6 do
Language check (page 49)
2 don't have to 3 must 4 needn't 5 didn't have to
6 ought to 7 need to 8 mustn't
Listening (page 50)
Ex 1: 2 false 3 true 4 true 5 false
Ex 2: See phrases in bold in audioscript
2 we all know about 3 I am sure you would agree that 4
surely that means that 5 we have to remember that 6 it is
obvious that
Writing (page 50) Suggested answer (54 words)
Dear Liz
I just wondered if you were free to help with a wildlife
campaign on Saturday? We're promoting a campaign to
protect the Asian elephant. Could you also see if anybody
else might be willing to join us? Can anybody interested
in helping give me a ring on 0114 257 8999?
Speak to you soon.
Anne
Reading (pages 50 and 51)
Ex 1: Campaigners disappointed
Ex 2: 2b 3f 4c 5a 6e
Ex 3: environmental, enthusiastic, ambitious, safety, risky,
excessive, original, alternative, competitive

Unit 13   Communications

Vocabulary (pages 52 and 53)
Ex 1: 2e 3a 4e 5b 6a
Ex 2: 2c/e 3a 4c/e 5d 6h 7f 8g
Ex 3: 2 announce 3 interruption 4 correspond
5 respond
Ex 4: 2 flow 3 voicemail 4 telecommunications
5 summarise 6 intrusive 7 policy 8 security
9 overload 10 transmit 11 deluge
Listening 1 (page 53)
Ex 2: – stress quick action to address the issue and put

things right
–find a way to turn any crisis into an opportunity
–finish any interview on a positive note

Language check (page 54)
Ex 1: 2 he could attend the training session. 3 the meeting wouldn't take long. 4 if she should book the conference room for 2pm. 5 he might have to leave early because of a doctor's appointment. 6 he was meeting Andy for lunch. 7 we had to be at the airport by 9.45. 8 me to take a break.
Ex 2: 2e 3a 4b 5f 6d 7g

Writing (page 54) Suggested answer (41 words)
Jamie
Susan Hill from Wantage Ltd phoned at 10am. Her train's delayed and she's running a little late for her meeting with you at 11. Please could you call her on her mobile. Her number's 07889 021021.
See you later.
Eric

Listening 2 (page 55)
Ex 1: 2b 3c 4a 5c 6c
Ex 2: Suggested answer
2 are perfect for building a corporate culture especially where employees rarely meet together in person.
3 the benefits are enormous – especially in a world that is changing.
4 that some people feel threatened by the democratising effect of new technology on communication.

Unit 14   Logistics

Language check (page 56)
Ex 1: Logistics in the past: companies used to guess what was in demand and supply this from existing stocks
Logistics now: more complex than in the past, uses new technology including the internet, uses just-in-time techniques for incoming and outgoing products, attempts to eliminate inventory, attempts to build to order rather than guessing what is in demand, comprehensive flexible freight operations, outsourcing of logistics to third parties
Ex 2: 2 is managed 3 is growing 4 open up 5 to be kept 6 were delivered 7 is done 8 goes 9 buy 10 is required 11 outsourcing 12 is forcing 13 has almost vanished

Vocabulary (page 57)
Ex 1: 2d 3e 4f 5a 6c
Ex 2: 2c 3b 4b 5a 6a 7b 8c 9b 10b
Ex 3: 2g 3f 4h 5e 6a 7d 8c
Ex 4: transport, run out of, track, scan, monitor

Reading (pages 58 and 59)
Ex 1: 2 Forrester (technology research firm) 3 Dell (computer maker) 4 Ford (car manufacturer) 5 Proctor & Gamble (consumer goods giant) 6 Nutech Solutions (software company)
Ex 2: 2 online 3 tested 4 suppliers 5 gains 6 goods 7 warehouses 8 chain
Ex 3: 2 false 3 true 4 false 5 true 6 false

Listening 1 (page 59)
Ex 2: 2d 3f 4a 5c 6g 7h 8e

Listening 2 (page 59)
2 catalogue 3 OU390 4 delivery

Writing (page 59) Suggested answer (55 words)
Dear Ms Reilly
In reply to your telephone enquiry, I am pleased to submit the following price information:
OU390 x 50 = £265.40.
This price includes VAT and the cost of delivery within the UK. We promise to deliver within two weeks of receiving an order.
I look forward to hearing from you.
Yours sincerely

Unit 15   Innovation

Vocabulary (page 60)
Ex 1: 2b 3c 4d 5c 6a
Ex 2: 2h 3a 4g 5c 6d 7f 8e
Ex 3: 2g 3a 4f 5i 6c 7j 8d 9e 10h

Reading (pages 61 and 62)
Ex 1: 2 true 3 true 4 false 5 false
Ex 2: 2 discovery 3 innovations 4 success 5 knowledge 6 application 7 investment 8 expiry/expiration 9 researchers 10 development
Ex 3: 2 failure 3 inadequacy 4 outside 5 winning 6 positive 7 huge 8 reduced

Language check (page 62)
Ex 1: 2 We should have patented our new process
3 we could have won the competition
4 You shouldn't have spent so much time
5 it might have been easier
6 What could I have done
Ex 2: Suggested answers
2 (He may) not have been responsible for it.
3 (I shouldn't) have eaten so much.
4 (I could) have written it quite easily.
5 (He might) have gone to the bank.
6 (we mightn't) have done what we did.
7 (He could) have come with us.
8 (We should) have been more conservative.
Ex 3: 2 How come you weren't able to complete the project on time? (C)
3 I'm really impressed by how you led the meeting. (P)
4 You've done a great job with the new range. (P)
5 I'm a little disappointed by your current performance. (C)
6 No-one could have done a better job. (P)

Listening (page 63)
Ex 1: Successful innovations: based on tried and tested technology, supported existing practices, met customers' needs, saved money
Less successful innovations: created with no clearly defined solution in mind, followed on from other people's work
Ex 2: A day-long discussion on the factors that promote successful innovation followed by the announcement of the winners of *The Economist's* Innovation Awards for this year
Ex 3: 2 on 3 in 4 about 5 to 6 by

Writing (page 63) Suggested answer (115 words)
Re: Economist Innovation Awards
Dear Sir/Madam
I am writing to nominate John Lee of Simple Solutions for an innovation award in the Energy category.
John has worked for many years on finding solutions to real needs which are cheap and simple while also being environmentally friendly. His latest success is the invention of a solar-driven power pack which can be attached to any bicycle. It not only uses a renewable energy source; it encourages people to stay on their bikes instead of choosing to travel by car. See the attached report for more details about John's inventions.
Please do not hesitate to contact me (kmichaels@simplesolutions.co.uk) for more information about John Lee.
Yours faithfully
Karl Michaels

Reading Test Part 1
1D 2B 3A 4D 5A 6C 7B

Reading Test Part 2
8E 9A 10C 11D 12F

Reading Test Part 3
13D 14C 15B 16A 17C 18B

Reading Test Part 4
19B 20C 21A 22B 23D 24C 25A 26D 27D 28A 29C 30A
31A 32D 33C

Reading Test Part 5
34 MORE 35 FOR 36 THEREFORE 37 SUCH 38 OF
39 CORRECT 40 SO 41 IT 42 CORRECT 43 THAT
44 THAN 45 CORRECT

Writing Test Part 1 Suggested answer (50 words)
Dear Jacob
I'm afraid I can't make the meeting you proposed on 4
August as I'm attending a conference that week. Would the
following week suit you? If so, what about 11 August at 10
am?
I look forward to hearing from you.
Best regards
Isabella

Writing Test Part 2 Suggested answer (120 words)
Dear Mr Davis
I saw your advertisement in The Economist and am
writing to request further information about the
offshoring services provided by OFT International.
I work for Blacks, a financial services company, and we
are interested in possibly outsourcing our administrative
services to India. We may also consider China and would
be keen to hear your views about the advantages of each
country.
We would particularly like to learn more about the
following:
–   your staff recruitment procedures
–   local costs compared with costs in this country
–   how best to identify suitable locations.
Could you also send me a price list regarding OFT
services? See my contact details below.
I look forward to learning more about OFT.
Yours sincerely
Geoff Childers

Listening Test Part 1
Conversation 1: 1 Team Leader 2 Customer Services
3 1(st) (of) May 4 communication
Conversation 2: 5 Chief Executive 6 accounting
7 potential risks 8 board
Conversation 3: 9 Macintyre 10 business plans
11 promotional strategy 12 customers

Listening Test Part 2
Section 1: 13F 14G 15C 16A 17B
Section 2: 18G 19E 20A 21F 22D

Listening Test Part 3
23B 24C 25A 26C 27A 28C 29B 30B